ADELPHI
Paper • 304

Iran–Saudi Arabia Relations and Regional Order

Contents

Oxford University Press, Great Clarendon Street, Oxford OX2 6DP

Oxford New York

Athens Auckland Bangkok Bombay
Calcutta Cape Town Dar es Salaam Delhi
Florence Hong Kong Istanbul Karachi
Kuala Lumpur Madras Madrid Melbourne
Mexico City Nairobi Paris Singapore
Taipei Tokyo Toronto
and associated companies in
Berlin Ibadan

Oxford is a trade mark of Oxford University Press

Published in the United States
by Oxford University Press Inc., New York

© The International Institute for Strategic Studies 1996

First published November 1996 by Oxford University Press for
The International Institute for Strategic Studies
23 Tavistock Street, London WC2E 7NQ

Director: Dr John Chipman
Deputy Director: Rose Gottemoeller

British Library Cataloguing in Publication Data

Data available

Library of Congress Cataloging in Publication Data

ISBN 0-19-829283-X
ISSN 0567-932X

INTRODUCTION

With the end of the Cold War, one of the key areas of continuing strategic interest is the Persian Gulf, where Iraq remains a marginal player in regional politics, Iran a potential threat and the Gulf Cooperation Council (GCC) states under Saudi Arabia's leadership largely reliant on external powers for their security. Those powers, particularly the United States, are growing increasingly sensitive to the manner in which domestic politics in the region, especially in Saudi Arabia and, differently, in Iran, can upset their strategic calculations. With growing international dependence on the region for oil supplies, increasing domestic pressure for change and the prospect of Iraq's eventual return to regional politics and the oil market, on what basis can regional security be constructed?

The relationship between Iran and Saudi Arabia is the key. Over the past 17 years, relations between these two states have been characterised by suppressed rivalry and distrust on several levels. Whether this can be transcended will depend in part on transformations within both countries as much as on the relationship itself, and is strongly influenced by the relations of both states with the United States. These asymmetries and differing priorities will set the parameters for cooperation in the Persian Gulf.

Better relations between Iran and Saudi Arabia could give the GCC a more useful function, for example, by balancing a potential threat from Iraq; by contrast, poor relations between them could produce a tactical alliance or *entente* between Iran and Iraq, complicating dual containment policies and putting pressure on the GCC. What would improved Iran–Saudi ties mean for security cooperation? Conversely, how would deteriorating relations between them affect regional security? Iran and Saudi Arabia are two parts of a triangle whose relations will influence and constrain the third part, Iraq. If there are limits to Iran–Saudi cooperation, are there equivalent limits to relations between Iran and Iraq or Saudi Arabia and Iraq? If no regional arrangement is likely, will the GCC's reliance on outside powers be sustainable?

This paper proposes that Iran–Saudi relations are constrained by a number of structural factors limiting significant security cooperation which have been exacerbated by the creation of the Islamic Republic of Iran (IRI) in 1979. Events since then have aggravated the threat from Iran and have increased mistrust. This situation may change if Iran transforms itself, but is unlikely to change enough for meaningful

3

cooperation in security affairs. Instead, a balance of power among the three principal Gulf states seems inevitable, and the stability of this balance will largely depend on the nature of domestic transformations within them.

The structural factors influencing Iran–Saudi relations include geopolitical differences, such as disparities in demography and geography, and consequent differing perspectives on regional issues. Questions about their respective influence in and leadership of Gulf affairs, oil issues and the role of outside powers compose the traditional 'national interest' agenda. National, cultural, ethnic and sectarian divisions in the region, such as between Persian and Arab, Shi'a and Sunni, aggravate the situation. The natural constituency and the relative weakness of the Arab Gulf states tend to 'Arabise' bilateral disputes, thus magnifying issues and polarising the region. For Iran, a dispute with any Arab neighbour risks becoming a dispute with all its Arab neighbours, infusing the situation with dramatic symbolism redolent of historical animosities.

To these structural factors have been added the particular challenges posed by the revolutionary IRI. As the only Shi'i state (the Shi'a constitute less than 15% of the Muslim world, and most live in Iran), its religious leaders claimed a broad Islamic sanction for their revolution. In offering it as a model for others and proclaiming a mission to extend true Islam to other states, Iran poses a direct threat to others in the Gulf and elsewhere. The Iranian government's claim to speak for a putative universal Islamic authority has been a clear challenge to the Saudi government which sees its legitimacy as tied to its role of protector of the Holy Places of Mecca and Medina.

Furthermore, Iran denounces Saudi Arabia as a client of the US – which Iran's revolutionary leaders have assigned a demonic role – claiming that the Saudi government takes instructions from Washington on a host of issues ranging from oil prices to the 'sell-out of Muslim interests in Palestine'. It charges Saudi Arabia with practising a passive, accommodating Islam at odds with Iran's militant support for Muslim rights everywhere. These accusations have produced a political tug of war that sets Shi'i Iran at odds with Wahabi Saudi Arabia. Iran has also questioned the compatibility of monarchy with true Islam.

Saudi Arabia has its own internal critics who accuse its rulers of being too accommodating to the West and insufficiently mindful of their Islamic obligations. Such criticism has been evident since the Kingdom was founded in the 1920s, and the June 1996 bombing of the US

4

military housing at Al-Khobar demonstrated that this strand of dissent is still very much alive. The emergence in 1979 of an Iranian regime dedicated to a populist, radical interpretation of those obligations and explicitly advocating a dramatic revision of the status quo alarmed the Saudi authorities. Not only were they being challenged regionally, but the nature of that challenge seemed likely to exacerbate internal divisions, both among the Shi'a of the Eastern Province and among Islamic radicals elsewhere in the Kingdom. By defining domestic and regional issues, alignments and leadership questions in Islamic terms, Iran served notice that it is a major regional player.

The advent of the IRI has been followed by a succession of related crises in the Gulf, notably the Iran–Iraq War, and the 1991 Gulf War between Iraq and the US-led allied coalition. Iran's foreign policy has been as much an expression of its revolutionary and Islamic impulses as of national interest, and its leaders have adjusted to these periods of crisis. By 1990–91, as Iran's regional fortunes were being revived by Saddam Hussein's blunder, there were pragmatic reasons for Saudi Arabia to seek some form of accommodation with Iran; there were also signs that this was reciprocated by elements within the Iranian leadership.

Any easing in tension, however, has not lasted, in part due to a weaker, split leadership presiding over a more divided Iranian nation. Increasingly, the strain between Islamic and revolutionary values and national interest has become more pronounced, but with economic stagnation and popular restlessness, renouncing such values may be problematic. While a more moderate policy *may* improve the economic situation, it may also exacerbate problems of legitimacy for the regime, especially among its die-hard faithful. By contrast, an activist foreign policy abroad might be used to excuse domestic failures and be justified as the price to be paid for adhering to its true values. Yet it appears unlikely that moderation in foreign policy will emerge in Iran separate from overall moderation.

Iran's erratic foreign policy reflects a divided leadership. In this regard, Saudi Arabia's special relations with the United States make Tehran's normalisation of relations with Riyadh especially sensitive. Iranian radicals see this as the beginning of a slippery slope to the renunciation of Iran's revolutionary and Islamic values, and to an eventual reconciliation with the United States. Iranian pragmatists see this as a natural response to changed circumstances which will enhance Iran's interests in the Persian Gulf.

There is substantial consensus within Iran that the country should play a leading role in the Persian Gulf, but there is much less on how it should play that role – whether in cooperation with or in opposition to the other littoral states. These divisions make it difficult for Tehran to formulate, let alone implement, a consistent policy and complicate Saudi Arabia's assessment of Iran's intentions. For example, while proclaiming a new era in relations with the Gulf states, Iran's policies on Islamic issues have not changed; it is, if anything, more militant on the issue of Palestine and more opposed to the current peace process today than it was in the 1980s. With increasing Saudi involvement in the peace process and its government's heightened concern to present a genuine Islamic image, this raises the question of whether Iran believes it can pursue normalisation with Riyadh in the Gulf while competing with it on Muslim issues further afield. It also raises the question of whether Iran has a grand strategy or whether its leaders are just reacting to shifts in domestic politics.

The Saudi view of Gulf security is dominated by its concern about the intentions of both Iran and Iraq. Faced with the need to ensure its own security, the Saudi government, under the direction of King Fahd, believes that it has found the answer in an ever closer relationship with the United States. Given the primacy of the US in Saudi security calculations, this is not a relationship that can be relinquished, nor is it something which the present Saudi monarch and defence establishment are prepared to downplay, either to improve relations with Iran or to placate domestic critics. This remains the case, despite decisions made in August 1996 to redeploy US forces based in the Kingdom to more remote locations. Iranian views of Gulf security stress the degree to which the US itself is not just an unwelcome presence, but a fundamental threat to Iran as well as the other Gulf states. For Tehran, the Saudi–US relationship remains a key challenge.

Both states recognise that there is another potential threat to Gulf security – Iraq. Iraq has always influenced the relations of the other two states and has played a role in their strategies. In the 1980s, Arab solidarity developed among the Gulf states in response to the perceived threat from Iran. In the first half of the 1990s, the Iraqi threat brought relations between Iran and the Arab Gulf states back into a formal equilibrium. The concern is now the way in which, eventually, Iraq will be slotted back into the balance. Will the region again be polarised, with Arabs facing Persians? Or will Iran join the GCC states in effectively containing Iraq?

On a different level, Iran's relations with the United States will affect Tehran's regional policies. Tehran's relations with Riyadh cannot change without reference to the relations each has with Washington. Iran–Saudi relations will therefore be influenced by relations between Iran and the US. To the degree that the US sees Iran as frustrating its special security relationship with Saudi Arabia, US–Iranian relations will automatically suffer. Hence, there is a potentially irreconcilable difference of views: Saudi Arabia looks to outside powers to balance the asymmetries within the Gulf itself, whereas Iran favours a 'Gulf-centred' view that excludes outsiders, precisely because of the role that would be offered to a country such as Iran. Whether this discrepancy in Saudi and Iranian views of Gulf security will prevent them establishing relatively cordial relations and the slow process of confidence-building is a key question in understanding the kind of regional order that may emerge.

There are pressures, both economic and international, on Iran to revise its goals, modulate its policies and reduce this rivalry. However, for the Iranian government to respond positively it would need to create a new domestic consensus which would sanction a much stronger line against those radical elements opposed to Iran becoming a 'normal', non-ideological state. It would also require a vision of regional security that is more cooperative and tolerant, and avoids the issue of its neighbours' domestic politics. At the present stage in Iran's political trajectory, it is difficult to see the government as having either the inclination or the authority to embark on such a course.

The Saudi government is not subject to similar pressures with regard to Iran, since the question of reconciliation with Iran does not occupy a parallel position in Saudi politics. Nor is there any expectation in Saudi Arabia that its government should play a role in Iranian society and politics. Rather, the government is expected to protect the state from threats such as those constituted by Iran, while guaranteeing political order. There are, of course, differences of opinion in Saudi Arabia about what this political order is. As a model, Iran plays only a minor role in such debates, but this does little to allay the Saudi authorities' fears. Not only does Iran use the same language of radical Islam as the Saudi regime's domestic Islamist critics, but many of the targets of their criticism are identical. In particular, the strong US–Saudi relationship has been attacked by both Iranian and Saudi dissidents, yet the relationship is seen by Saudi authorities as a fundamental guarantee of their security, in large part against the perceived threat from Iran.

Consequently, relations between Iran and Saudi Arabia are vulnerable to changes within Iran, as well as to heightened Saudi sensitivities when domestic dissent is on the rise.

In part, therefore, regional order in the Persian Gulf is a function of domestic political developments in Iran and Saudi Arabia. In both cases, the regimes are understandably if perhaps unduly sensitised to each other in ways which make close relations difficult to establish and sustain, regardless of the practical benefits that might stem from such cooperation. Weaknesses in the dual form of government that exists in Iran, or the anxieties of the Al Saud at the appearance of any domestic opposition, are capable of disrupting relations between the two states. In some measure this sensitivity is due to the part played by the US in maintaining regional order. The actual power of the US in the Gulf is seen in diametrically opposite ways by Tehran and Riyadh – for Iran it constitutes a military threat; for Saudi Arabia it is the best guarantee of its military security. Inevitably, therefore, US policy not only in the Gulf, but also elsewhere in the Middle East will have an impact on Iranian–Saudi relations. For Iran to cooperate with Saudi Arabia on matters of regional security it would need to accept the role of the US in the Gulf, which is improbable under present circumstances. It is all the more important, therefore, to understand the processes which contribute to the deterioration in relations and the likelihood of constructing some form of regional order with the elements that are currently in place.

I. THE RECORD OF RELATIONS 1979–1991

Gulf Security During the Iran–Iraq War

From the British departure from the Persian Gulf in December 1971 until the revolution in Iran in February 1979, Iran and Saudi Arabia managed their mutual relations without incident. In the 1960s, the two pro-Western monarchs coordinated their policies in the face of the mutually sensed threat from Abdul Nasser's Egypt to the Arabian peninsula and Persian Gulf. Even then, with parallel security concerns and no religious leadership rivalry, Iran and Saudi Arabia were unable to move beyond a stiff cordiality. Although they settled a number of potentially contentious bilateral issues (the disposition of the Farsi and Arabi islands and the demarcation of the continental shelf), there was a gap between the two states that made cooperation difficult.

In the 1970s, when Iran sought to organise the region for cooperation on security, it found the Saudis reluctant and jealous of its ties with neighbours such as Oman and Dubai. Iran under the Shah concluded that the Saudis were unwilling to be junior partners and unable to be equal partners. It therefore ceased the quest for a regional approach, concentrating instead on bilateral relationships. A common alignment with the West and shared conservatism could not translate into practical cooperation. Iranian and Saudi spheres of interest were not identical and, although the Gulf was important for both of them, it was not the only area of mutual interest. However, the Saudi government had no difficulty reconciling the generally placatory government of the Shah with its other concerns and this conciliatory mood helped reduce the occasional friction which arose.

Revolutionary Iran was a different matter. In the first decade after the revolution Iran left a trail of devastation in its regional relations, littered with spontaneous utterances and unfettered intervention in neighbouring states, upsetting in a few months the confidence that had taken years of diplomacy to build.

Nowhere was this more apparent than in Saudi Arabia. The spectacle and rhetoric of the Iranian revolution alarmed many in Saudi Arabia and disconcerted then Crown Prince Fahd, who had cultivated a relationship with the Shah and with whom he shared a pro-Western outlook. However, there were others in Saudi Arabia's ruling circles, most notably Prince Abdullah and some of the sons of the late King Faisal, who did not see the revolution in Iran as necessarily inimical to Saudi interests. They derived two lessons from the revolution which were indirect indictments of current Saudi policy: the inevitable counter-reaction of an Islamic society if subjected to rapid and insensitive modernisation on the Western model, and the unreliability of the US as an ally, given the speed with which it abandoned the Shah.

Whilst a more conciliatory attitude in Saudi Arabia might have pleased the Bazargan government, the dynamics of revolutionary politics did not allow this. Regionally, Saudi Arabia moved closer to Iraq as the only credible local military deterrent to Iranian ambitions. In the summer of 1979, it initiated talks on military and security cooperation with the smaller Gulf states, many of which felt vulnerable to Iranian threats. On the international level, the Carter 'doctrine' and the formation of the US Central Command were welcomed by Fahd and others.

The outbreak in 1980 of the Iran–Iraq War was seen by Iranians as an attempt by Iraq and its allies, Saudi Arabia and the West, to snuff out the revolution. To Iran, the silence of the UN about the Iraqi attack, the emergence of the other Arab Gulf states as virtual co-belligerents with Iraq, and the eventual entry of the United States into the war on Iraq's side were evidence enough to sustain this thesis. For the purposes of this paper, it is important to note how the experience of eight years of war affected Iranian thinking and how the lessons learned from it applied to their relations with Saudi Arabia.

Iran viewed the Iraqi attack as unprovoked and premeditated and Arab support for it as evidence of hostility; it saw itself as the aggrieved party. This was not diminished by Saudi Arabia's 'explanation' that its support for Iraq had been 'dictated by Arab and Islamic ties and imposed by neighbourliness'.[1] There is a strong possibility that Fahd and others in Saudi Arabia had foreknowledge of the invasion, even if they did not necessarily share the Iraqi regime's optimistic – and unrealistic – assessment of what that invasion could achieve. Nevertheless, once the war had begun, the Saudis and others in the Gulf hoped that Iran would at least be humbled and understand the limits of its power, thus checking any tendency to encroach upon the Gulf states and the Arab world in the name of 'Islamic revolution'.

It rapidly became clear that Saddam Hussein had failed in his original intention. This led to understandable concern and alarm in Saudi Arabia, particularly in view of the fact that the Iranian Navy and Air Force were still more or less intact. Potentially, the military and economic security of the Kingdom was at risk and there was little or nothing that either Iraq or Saudi Arabia itself could do. It was in the light of these concerns that Fahd turned to the US and initiated the negotiations which led to the massive Airborne Warning and Control System (AWACS) deal of 1980–81. This agreement was significant in that it required an unprecedented degree of direct US involvement and the presence of US military personnel in Saudi Arabia.

At the same time, Saudi Arabia launched a mediation initiative to end the war through the Islamic Conference Organisation (ICO). Although Iran responded relatively favourably to the resolutions of the Ta'if conference in 1981, this process became subject to the vicissitudes of Iranian domestic, revolutionary politics. With the ousting of President Bani Sadr in June 1981, the plan came to naught; thereafter, the Saudi government lent its weight to any UN or Arab League initiative that seemed likely to persuade Iran to accept a cease-fire. These initiatives, however, generally condemned Iran's conduct of the war and its refusal to accept the terms of the UN cease-fire resolution. To the Iranian government, this Saudi behaviour looked less like attempted mediation than partisanship.

Saudi Arabia also took advantage of the war to formalise its increasingly close relations with the smaller Arab Gulf states, which led to the creation of the GCC, excluding both Iran and Iraq, in May 1981. Iran saw the Council as a vehicle for Saudi domination of the Arabian peninsula.[2] The GCC enhanced internal security cooperation and provided a legitimate device for calling in outside assistance. Both of these functions were responses to perceived threats – both internal and external – from Iran.

However, the increasingly close relationship between Saudi Arabia and the US proved to be of greatest significance for the Iranian–Saudi relationship.[3] By inviting the United States into the Gulf to provide military assistance, Saudi Arabia started a process that was to lead to military – primarily naval – engagements, culminating in the loss of civilian lives in the destruction of an Iranian airliner in 1988. To Iran, Saudi Arabia's palpable dependence on Washington was a manifest reason for concern. In 1984, Saudi aircraft, using AWACS information, shot down two Iranian planes, accusing them of encroaching on its territorial waters. Iran's reaction was restrained. For Fahd, now King of Saudi Arabia, this was a dramatic vindication of the policy he initiated in the early 1980s; thanks to the modernisation of the Saudi Air Force and US assistance, Iran was made aware of the limits of its power.

These incidents gave both the Iranian and Saudi governments reason to open a dialogue. For its part, the Saudi government was keen to persuade Iran to accept the terms of a cease-fire. The war, by moving from the apparent stalemate on the land front between Iran and Iraq, looked set to spread destructively to the shipping lanes of the Gulf, thereby threatening the economic interests of Saudi Arabia and its GCC allies very directly. At the same time, Iran emerged from its self-absorption to recognise the need for an 'open door' policy towards its neighbours; however, none of this seemed to produce concrete results. Iran was unable to sustain an interest in diplomacy and its opening appeared tactical rather than indicative of a changed course. Iran wanted to continue war 'until victory' and its successful offensive at Faw in early 1986 seemed to presage precisely such a victory, giving it little incentive to negotiate. Meanwhile, the Arab states saw no reason for contrition once the Western states had taken their side.

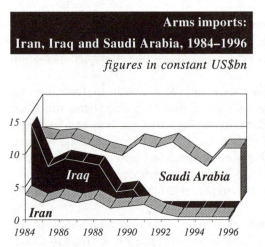

**Arms imports:
Iran, Iraq and Saudi Arabia, 1984–1996**

figures in constant US$bn

Note 1995 and 1996 figures are preliminary estimates
Source US Arms Control and Disarmament Agency, World Military Expenditures and Arms Transfers, 1995

Iran's apparent incomprehension of the insecurities which drove Saudi Arabia into virtual alignment with the US is more understandable if seen from Iran's perspective – the war was a defensive one in which other states joined with the aggressor, Iraq. While Iran was cut off from military supplies, Saudi military expenditures in the 1980s outstripped those of both Iran and Iraq.[4] Iran's military purchases, driven by its war needs, were modest and amounted to an attempt to replace arms lost or consumed – often with inferior weapons purchased at inflated prices. Iran's acquisition of missiles in 1985–86 was a response to Iraq's use of missiles against the frontier region from the outset of the war. Iran never directly threatened Saudi Arabia militarily, although it attacked Saudi-bound tankers in response to Iraqi attacks on its oil exports. This was intended to pressure Iraq to stop the 'tanker war', not to destabilise Saudi Arabia. This was not, though, how the Saudi government viewed the matter and, in the last years of the war, there was a noticeable hardening of Saudi policy.

The Iranians were frustrated at being depicted as a regional menace while the Arab states armed and funded Iraq, invited outside powers into the Gulf, stocked up on arms that in other hands would be called 'destabilising' and kept silent on, if they did not commend, Iraq's use of chemical weapons. On the diplomatic front, too, Iran felt pressure. Saudi Arabia used the war to dominate the GCC. Between the two Gulf wars Iran attempted to improve relations with these individual states but was stymied by the Saudis who had severed diplomatic relations with Tehran in 1988 and with whom there were few contacts during these years.[5]

Iraq's invasion of Kuwait in 1990 took Saudi Arabia and the rest of the GCC by surprise. However, the crisis did offer the opportunity for some form of Saudi–Iranian *rapprochement*, if not reconciliation. In Iran's view, of course, Saudi policy had made Saddam's second aggression much easier – it had armed him, minimised his threat and prevented the establishment of a regional balance. The Saudi government did not think that any degree of normalisation with Iran would compromise the US connection, which had become much more important since then. Despite these issues, high-level contacts were re-established with Iran during this time and, although it was certainly premature to speak of the creation of 'a new regional security system'[6] it did allow two sides of the triangle to hold an increasingly reassuring dialogue over the prostrate form of the third.

The Oil Dimension
There were two elements to the oil issue in the Iran–Iraq War. The first concerned the passage of oil through the Gulf. When Iran blocked Iraq's maritime exports, Saudi Arabia facilitated oil exports through overland pipelines on its territory. When Iraq bombed Iranian tankers in 1984, Tehran retaliated against third parties, mainly Arab states, trying to dissuade them from assisting Baghdad and encouraging them to urge restraint. Iran's position was that if its oil exports were stopped, those of others would be as well. It had every interest in the free flow of oil and none in blocking exports (save those of Iraq). Led by Saudi Arabia, the Arab states helped Iraq internationalise the war, inviting in foreign navies essentially to neutralise Iran's maritime advantage and reduce their own vulnerability. Iran responded by mining the waters of the

Gulf. Saudi Arabia's policy in this part of the war was unfriendly and clearly damaging to Iranian interests. Saudi Arabia, like the other GCC states, was greatly influenced by the US view that Iran posed a potential threat to navigation – as if Iran itself did not rely almost exclusively on the Gulf for its own exports.

In the other area, oil production and pricing, Iran saw Saudi Arabia as even more hostile. In essence, Saudi Arabia boosted its own production when there were shortfalls at the beginning of the war and later cut back its production to maintain prices in the face of an oil glut. Thus, from a level of about ten million barrels per day (mb/d) in 1981, Saudi production fell to 2 mb/d in 1985. King Fahd was under great pressure from the ruling family to abandon the policy of making Saudi Arabia the 'swing producer' of the Organization of Petroleum Exporting Countries (OPEC). As a result, Saudi Arabia decided in 1986 to step up production in the belief that this would 'discipline' the other members of OPEC and convince them to cut back their own production. The strategy backfired and led to a collapse in oil prices, harming all oil producers, including Saudi Arabia, as well as Iran. Iran's frustration led it to view OPEC as 'an agency of Saudi Arabia' which was acting as 'an enemy and archrival.'[7]

In 1986–87 Iran's oil revenues dropped drastically to an estimated $6.8 billion from $21.2bn in 1983–84.[8] One Iranian scholar referred to the 'Saudi-engineered oil glut' as 'treason'.[9] He also argued that Saudi oil power served Western interests and undermined revolutionary Iran.[10]

Both Saudi Arabia and Iran had an interest in maximising their oil revenues, but each had very different strategies to that end. Moreover, Saudi strategy went directly against Iran's interests and, with the hardening of Saudi attitudes, it seemed to Tehran as if Saudi Arabia was waging economic warfare. Saudi Arabia's capacity and willingness both to undermine Iran's source of income and to buttress its adversary's needs financially and diplomatically made Iran realise the degree to which OPEC had become a Saudi-dominated institution. Once the Saudis took a position there was little that Iran could do to change it. Equally, when Saudi Arabia chose, it could hurt Iran economically, politically and domestically through the its decisions on oil pricing and production.

The Islamic Dimension: The *Hajj* and the Shi'a
Revolutionary Iran's aspiration to play a leading role in Islam has brought it into direct conflict with Saudi Arabia.[11] This rivalry

embraces sectarian questions as well as political issues such as alignment with the United States. Iran's challenge, even if presented in Islamic guise, was a political one. Ayatollah Khomeini's activist Islam was anti-monarchical, anti-Western and pitted Iran against the House of Saud in the Gulf and in the Islamic world as a whole. Iran's activism in the Muslim world – among the Palestinians and in Lebanon and Afghanistan – became part of a broader rivalry for influence.[12] Whereas Saudi Arabia had the resources and control of Islamic institutions (like the ICO), Iran in the 1980s offered a dynamic policy agenda and potential support for the foot soldiers of Islam.

However, Iran was unable to transcend the 'Shi'i ghetto' (in Olivier Roy's phrase) – the sectarian divide in the Islamic world. In Lebanon it supported the Shi'a through *Hizbollah*; in Afghanistan it supported the Shi'i group, *Hezb e Wahdat*. Iran found it difficult to make headway with secular Palestinian groups like the Palestine Liberation Organization (PLO). Even where the Shi'a were numerous, or a majority, as in Iraq and Bahrain, the 'tenacity of ethnicity, nationalism, sectarianism in the Middle East ... was a serious blow to Iran's Islamic universalism'.[13] Indeed, Khomeini's discourse and emphasis had, within five years, 'widened the gap between the predominantly Shi'i population of Iran and Sunni majorities elsewhere ... and exacerbated sectarian feeling throughout the Muslim world'.[14]

Khomeini's revolution presented a potential threat to all Arab Gulf states with Shi'i populations in that it could inspire similar militancy against what might be seen as oppressive governments; however, it did not want to limit its potential constituency to the Shi'i world, a minority in Islam. Rather, it preached a highly politically charged Islamic universalism, pitting a populist Islam of the 'oppressed' (*mustazefin*) against the 'oppressors' (*mustakbarin*), namely conservative, establishment Islam, represented by Saudi Arabia.[15] Iran's style of Islam was revolutionary, militantly anti-Western and activist, and was to clash repeatedly with Saudi Islam which pragmatically sought to use religion to bolster the status quo. A key problem for Iran's neighbours was that however much it sought to depict its intentions as strictly religious, behind its denials of any intent to export the revolution were the realities of Iranian state power, and even more of Iranian national interest. Iran regarded Saudi Arabia as 'the arch agent of the "Great Satan" whose Gulf policy is condemned in every respect'.[16] This was a political judgement based on Iran's national interest, notwithstanding Tehran's attempt to depict the US as the enemy of Islam.

If Iran initially relied on the force of its model to inspire other Muslims and especially Shi'a, it soon moved to direct intervention.[17] Shortly after Iran's revolution, some Shi'a of Saudi Arabia's Eastern Province set up *Munazama Al-Thawra Al-Islamiyya li-l-Tahrir Al-Jazira Al-Arabiyya* (the Islamic Revolution Organisation for the Liberation of the Arabian Peninsula) which became involved, often in association with secular dissidents, in various anti-regime activities in Saudi Arabia and in the Middle East. These activities never amounted to much – occasional attacks on Saudi diplomats or buildings abroad and limited acts of sabotage within Saudi Arabia. Nevertheless, the nature of these activities and the mood of the times were seen as symptomatic of something much more dangerous and as an indication of a concerted Iranian strategy of subversion. There were periodic detentions and interrogations of considerable numbers of people suspected of involvement in these activities, especially during the period 1981–85. Most of the arrests were made in the Eastern Province, although others suspected of belonging to Islamic and non-Islamic political associations were also detained. By 1986, it was estimated that there were about 900 political prisoners in Saudi Arabia.[18]

During the same period, Iran was suspected of complicity in subversion in Bahrain in 1981 and in Kuwait in 1983 and 1985, accused of supporting such groups as the Islamic Front for the Liberation of Bahrain. It trained, funded and organised clandestine groups, distributed pamphlets and broadcast inflammatory propaganda. These events prompted Saudi Arabia to conclude bilateral security agreements with Bahrain in 1981 (and subsequently with most of its fellow GCC members) and prompted the Saudi Interior Minister Prince Nayef to refer to Iran as the 'Gulf's terrorists'.[19] Thereafter, in the war with Iraq, the Gulf states judged Iran's war aims against its record of interference in its neighbours' affairs.

Partly in response to Iran's activity, and partly in response to forces at work within Saudi society itself, King Fahd, since his accession in 1982, had cultivated his own image as a pious Islamic monarch, determined to enforce the *shari'a*, to advance the Wahabi 'call' and to protect the Holy Places. He instituted a weekly meeting with the *'ulama* (Islamic jurists), reorganised and reactivated the *mutawwi'in* (sometimes called the 'religious police'), re-emphasised the role of the Islamic authorities in the educational system and re-invigorated the Directorate for Islamic Propagation. In 1986 he officially decreed that he should henceforth be referred to not as *Jallalatuh* (His Majesty) (the term in Arabic has close and, some would say, impious association with one of the attributes of God), but rather as *Khadim Al-Haramayn Al-Sharifayn* (servant of the two Holy Places). There were sound domestic reasons for these moves, but they were also a clear sign that the Saudi ruling family felt it necessary to reassert its own Islamic credentials in the face of the constant public challenge from Iran. Foremost among these has been Iranian-sponsored activities in relation to the annual *Hajj* pilgrimage.

Indeed, the *Hajj* issue between Iran and Saudi Arabia has been a constant source of tension in the 17 years since the revolution. In the early years, when the Iranian revolution still had momentum and widespread attraction as a model, Saudi Arabia found it difficult to resist Iran's demands to hold demonstrations during the course of the pilgrimage. It felt too vulnerable politically *vis-à-vis* Iran and possibly its own Shi'i community to block these rallies. Over time, having sided with Iraq during the war with Iran, and having invested more resources in its neglected Shi'i areas, Saudi Arabia became more confident and willing to resist Iran.

In 1987, a major incident turned into tragedy when some 450 pilgrims, principally Iranian, were killed by Saudi security forces in confused circumstances. Understandably, this incident led to a spate of accusations between the two governments as each tried to place the blame for the tragedy on the other. Saudi Arabia thereafter sought to limit the number of Iranian pilgrims to 45,000 (hitherto the Iranian pilgrims had numbered over 150,000). It also placed an absolute ban on further demonstrations, which Iran resisted. Negotiations on these topics came to naught and, possibly to provoke an Iranian boycott of the *Hajj*, Saudi Arabia simply severed diplomatic relations with Tehran in April 1988. Ties remained cut for three years, and during this period the Iranians did indeed boycott the *Hajj*, but there were still problems. In 1989, two explosions near the Grand Mosque in Mecca were attributed to a group of Kuwaiti Shi'a, mostly of Iranian origin, 16 of whom were executed for their part in the bombing.

The recurrence and continuing centrality of this issue in Iran's relations with Saudi Arabia can be appreciated best by recognising its symbolic, as well as religious and political, dimensions. For Iran, the *Hajj* remains an ideal stage for demonstrating its continued political vitality and a potent instrument for undermining Saudi Arabia by denouncing its allies and underscoring its passivity. For Saudi Arabia, although the appeal of Iran may have diminished, the risk of political upheaval and instability has not, and the Kingdom still fears Iran's capacity for subversion. Thus, although the issue is phrased in religious terms, the underlying tensions and recriminations are political.

Regional Security

The cease-fire with Iraq in mid-1988 ushered in a period of stocktaking and self-criticism in Iran. Iran sought to rebuild with the Arab states the bridges that had been damaged during eight years of war. It encountered considerable scepticism, especially in Saudi Arabia. By mid-1990, a year after Khomeini's death and before Saddam's attack on Kuwait, Iranian efforts to renew ties with Saudi Arabia accelerated. Even then, Iran appeared ambivalent about Saudi Arabia. While the country's spiritual leader (Rahbar) Ayatollah Ali Khamene'i was referring to the 'tyrannical and corrupt Saudi leaders' who had prevented denunciation of the US and Israel, President Hashemi Rafsanjani was telling Iranian diplomats that Iran's policy was to have good relations with its neighbours, for the 'extension of regional cooperation in political, economic and cultural dimensions'.[20]

Iran's barbed overtures reflected a change – or at least variation – in tone. The end of the war with Iraq, the death of Khomeini and the appearance of a more pragmatic approach seemed to usher in a new era, although doubts about Iran's sincerity remained. In particular, the Saudi government appeared disappointed that Khomeini's death had not produced the clear cut change in Iranian regional policies that it had hoped would emerge. As in previous years, relations between the two states fluctuated between conciliatory noises or gestures and fully-fledged campaigns of vitriolic propaganda, as well as suspected direct moves to harm each other's interests. These were temporarily submerged, however, by Iraq's seizure of Kuwait. Iran was thus given a new opportunity to improve relations with the Gulf states.

What lessons had been learnt since 1979? Some of Iran's leaders recognised that its belligerent tone had contributed to its own isolation in the Gulf. This was implicit in the new policy of 'not making enemies unnecessarily'.[21] But were they prepared in the interests of pragmatic cooperation to drop their ideological views and build the confidence necessary for regional cooperation? Tehran concluded from the events of the 1980s that Iran could no longer be ignored, that there could be no security in the Persian Gulf *without* its active participation. Similarly, in its view, regional security *with* the presence of outside powers was a contradiction in terms.[22]

Iran's approach – to oppose outside powers' participation in regional security – went counter to the interests of the Arab states. It underestimated the traumas that two major crises had inflicted on these states, and the sense of threat they felt from both Iran and Iraq. It understated the degree to which its own contradictory statements and fluctuations in policy undermined rather than instilled confidence. Iran also misread the degree to which Saudi Arabia distrusted the Islamic Republic and the amount of time and effort that would be needed to repair the damage. While Iran believed it could capitalise on the threat from Iraq to improve its relations with the GCC states, the Saudis remained sceptical.[23] Iran thus relied on its own centrality and failed to maintain a consistent and moderate policy line.

For the Saudis, the Iran–Iraq War and the dangers represented by the Iranian revolution reinforced their decision to develop the GCC as an internal security mechanism, whilst relying increasingly on Western, and particularly US, assistance for protection against direct military threats. Iran's erratic behaviour towards Saudi Arabia during the war years, alternating threats with conciliatory noises, left the Saudi government perplexed about the true direction of Iranian policy. It also left the Saudis mistrustful of any professed commitment to non-interference in the affairs of others, to peaceful cooperation or to the establishment of a 'security partnership' in the Gulf.

However, the strategy of helping Iraq build its armed forces and of encouraging direct US involvement in the war appeared to have been vindicated by Iran's acceptance of the cease-fire terms in 1988. No amount of persuasion or mediation had succeeded prior to this. It seemed to suggest to the Saudis that they needed to ensure that a substantial counter-force stood ready to support them in their dealings with Iran in the future. However, Saddam Hussein's behaviour in 1990 (if not before) persuaded the Saudi government that Iraq could scarcely be relied upon to play this role. Similarly, it would have been inconceivable to have expected Iran to assist Saudi Arabia in dealing with the kind of threat represented by Iraq in 1990. In these circumstances, the advantages of the US protective shield far outweighed its disadvantages for Saudi Arabia. The willingness of the US to play such a role constituted the 'realities' of Gulf security from the Saudi perspective. Acceptance of such a perspective and its underlying priorities would test the limits of the Iranian leadership's pragmatism in seeking to establish good relations with Saudi Arabia in the 1990s.

II. CONTEMPORARY QUESTIONS OF SECURITY

Military Threat Perceptions and Responses

From Iran's vantage point, the most striking feature of the post-Cold War world is the dominant position of the United States. The US can now pursue policies, such as the Middle East peace process, relatively uncontested. It can target adversaries and selectively punish them with sanctions, although the effects of these are often limited. Iran faces an international order dominated by economic power, of which it has little, with more emphasis on regional politics, which it now conducts with few, if any, allies.

While the rift between the Arab and Persian shores of the Gulf grew in the 1980s, Iraq's aggression against Kuwait gave Iran a reprieve. Without effacing the memory of Iran as a potential threat, it gave Tehran a chance to redefine its interests and integrate itself into Persian Gulf politics. With Iraq ostracised from Gulf politics, Iran's importance was correspondingly enhanced. However, this windfall came with a catch: the United States also gained as a result of the 1991 Gulf War and its position in the region was strengthened. The Arab Gulf states were less reticent about enhancing their security ties with the US. The US in turn increased and made more permanent its military presence in the region (amounting to some 20,000 personnel, 200 aircraft and 20 surface vessels at any given time).

The lessons of the two Gulf wars were stark and vivid for Iran. They demonstrated the importance of military professionalism and competence, the advantages of deploying modern weapons systems, and the vulnerability of expensive infrastructures to accurate air strikes. The US has continued to show its readiness to punish the regime in Baghdad with long-range attacks. In view of the US military presence, tensions with Washington and Iran's own vulnerability, Iran was concerned that these strikes might not in future be limited only to Iraq.[1] Indeed, in August 1996, US officials began to talk openly of attacks against Iran if it were found to be complicit in terrorist activities against US citizens, whether in Saudi Arabia or elsewhere. Quite apart from the threat implied, the United States' military forces acted to frustrate Iran's sense of importance as the largest regional state. For Iran, a strengthened US presence distorted the natural order of regional relationships.

This view was based on a sense of weakness rather than strength. The war with Iraq and international isolation cost Iran dearly. It had lost or run down most of its military equipment, which was becoming obsolescent, and it was unable to acquire spare parts or upgrades from the West that might extend the lives of its key weapons systems. Iran's land forces were in disarray, its air defences virtually non-existent and its air force in the throes of a major change to a totally new supplier – Russia. The difficulties of Iran's revolutionary leaders moving from one set of systems to another involves a host of problems in language, logistics, maintenance, training, doctrine and overall assimilation, all of which limit effectiveness for a number of years. In Iran's case, the problem was compounded by the switch from advanced to less advanced technology, by the absence of a reliable supplier (given the turmoil in the Russian arms industries), by an ideological predisposition to emphasise domestic production and by financial constraints. Iran is also attempting to reorganise its armed forces, emphasising professionalism over ideological considerations and manoeuvre over a static approach to warfare.

Inferences about Iran's intentions from its pattern of military procurement need to be drawn with caution. This procurement is influenced as much by lessons derived from the war with Iraq and the availability of arms as by any strategic grand design. Similarly, budgets rather than strategy dictate the pace of the arms programme and, given reliance on oil revenues which fluctuate widely, that pace is bound to be uncertain and variable. (For example the third *Kilo*-class submarine has yet to be delivered to Iran from Russia because of Iran's financial problems.)

Iran's annual defence expenditure has been modest compared to that of Saudi Arabia, which has less than a third of Iran's population and a less varied set of security concerns (for Iran has to consider not only Iraq but also its unstable northern and eastern borders). Considering that Saudi Arabia consistently outspent Iran militarily during the years of the Iran–Iraq war, Iran's view that its own arms purchases are necessary and minimal while those of Saudi Arabia are unusually large is not surprising.[2] Also, given the coalition's reliance in *Operation Desert Storm* on the infrastructure in place in Saudi Arabia, Iranian planners must consider whether Saudi arms purchases are intended solely for their own use.[3]

From these same perspectives, the United States' formulation in May 1993 of a 'dual containment' policy towards Iraq and Iran bears a striking similarity to the Saudi ideal: the exclusion of the two major Gulf powers and concentration on the centrality of the Kingdom in regional affairs. In this view, the United States and Saudi Arabia have several reasons for exaggerating the threat posed to the region by Iran.

- Such a threat rationalises the massive transfer of arms when such costs are causing concern in certain Arab Gulf states.
- In Iran's view, it opens the door to the 'selective proliferation' of arms that require US transfers, but brands those destined for Iran (or Iraq) as inherently destabilising.
- It also keeps the GCC together, close to Saudi Arabia and dependent on the US for security, whose presence is thereby justified.[4] Iran registered 'extreme concern' when Kuwait concluded a ten year defence cooperation agreement with the US in late 1991. It similarly opposed subsequent agreements with other Gulf states.

The United States has drawn public attention to Iran's alleged military build-up, including chemical weapons, on and around Abu Musa island.[5] It has repeatedly declared that Iran is aggressively pursuing weapons of mass destruction (WMD), including nuclear weapons,[6] and has leaked reports that in straitened economic circumstances Iran might resort to aggression, block the flow of oil and seize Arab territory.[7] Iran is concerned that the aim of US allegations and Israeli threats regarding the impermissibility of Iran acquiring nuclear weapons is to justify a preventive attack on its facilities and infrastructure.[8]

Iran's attitude towards the US presence in the Gulf has evolved as relations have become more strained. In March 1991, Rafsanjani characterised the presence as giving rise to tension, but not constituting a threat.[9] By 1994–95, Iran's attitude had changed and warnings (and protests to the UN) about the US military presence in the Gulf had become more frequent, with one leader calling it a 'stupid show of strength'.[10]

Iranian military exercises anticipate and plan for the possible use of force by the US in several of the following scenarios:

- an attack (unilaterally or with Israel) against it; the targets may be production facilities of nuclear or other WMDs, research facilities or sites housing relevant technology.
- punitive strikes against military and/or infrastructure targets. These might be retaliatory strikes for participation in terrorism or warning strikes for supporting terrorist groups or opposing the peace process.
- US assistance to an Arab state in support of its claims in a territorial dispute with Iran, such as to the United Arab Emirates

(UAE) over Abu Musa. In this case, US forces might launch a surprise attack and occupy the island, thereby creating a difficult-to-reverse *fait accompli*.

In none of these cases would the United States act alone; in all scenarios, regional states would be implicated in some way. Consequently, Iranian strategy revolves around deterring a US attack and preventing assistance by regional states. Iran might target the key state, Saudi Arabia, and in effect hold it hostage. Iran could threaten to respond against Saudi oil facilities (15 minutes' flight time from Iranian bases) if it were attacked. Long-range missiles might be the preferred weapon for this scenario.

A related strategy would be to deter or inhibit the entry of the US Navy into the Persian Gulf in times of crisis. This would be consistent with the acquisition and deployment of missiles, mines and submarines. But these weapons are more impressive as threats than in actual use. In any case, most US naval operations against Iran could be conducted from ships stationed outside Gulf waters. Blocking the entrance to the Gulf would also harm Iran, since with no overland pipeline routes for its oil exports it is more dependent on the flow of oil through the Gulf than Saudi Arabia or other regional states.

In trying to impress the Arab states of the Persian Gulf, Iran has to avoid frightening them off. This nuance is not easy for a state which has many contradictory inclinations and pronouncements. Iran must convince its neighbours not to ignore it without actually threatening them. To improve and emphasise its military preparedness Iran undertakes a regular series of military exercises which include amphibious forces, missile forces and combined arms in both the northern and southern Gulf.

In April 1994, Iran offered to hold joint land exercises with its Gulf neighbours. Kuwait responded in August that it would consider the offer and submit it to the GCC. In September 1994 Iran's Foreign Minister proposed at the Conference on Disarmament in Geneva the conclusion of a 'defensive security pact' among the littoral states of the Gulf. This included the suggestion that all states should become parties to the Nuclear Non-Proliferation Treaty and the Chemical Weapons Convention and that provisions for inspections and monitoring of nuclear, chemical and biological weapons be undertaken on a regional basis. Regarding conventional weapons, Iran called for a limit to military expenditures, a ceiling on arms imports and information exchanges to improve transparency.[11] This offer has not been elaborated further, but remains on the table until political relations make cooperation easier.

Yet Saudi Arabia is perplexed by Iran's intentions. As one Saudi paper put it in 1993, 'The passage of time has actually increased the unclear nature of the picture *vis-à-vis* its relations with neighbours', stating that the Saudi hope was to 'persuade Iran to make its relations with all the region's states clear and coherent without resorting to duality, telling the Iranian scene one thing and its neighbours another'.[12] It is partly for this reason that Saudi Arabia and the other Gulf states have pressed ahead, taking unilateral measures to ensure their own military security, generally in close collaboration with the US and other Western states. For all the improvement in relations between Iran and Saudi Arabia as a result of the Iraqi invasion of Kuwait and the subsequent defeat of Iraq, Iran has done nothing since to justify a fundamental revision of Saudi threat perceptions or defence strategies.

Saudi strategy remains largely geared to deterring aggression – principally from Iraq or Iran – and in this the US has a central role to play. Even before the bombs which were targeted at the US military presence in the Kingdom, the Saudi government was well aware of less conventional threats to its security, such as domestic reaction against a government that is too close to the West and to the US in particular. It also recognises the possibility of an increasingly disaffected officer corps should the expansion of the Saudi armed forces outstrip existing forms of supervision and control. At the same time, the King must cultivate the consensus of the ruling family's senior princes, not all of whom are convinced that a strong public defence association with the US is the best guarantee of Saudi Arabian security.

Subsequent to Iraq's defeat in 1991, the Saudi government had to decide how best to defend of the Kingdom. Possibly impressed by the size of the Iraqi armed forces and by the size of the allied force assembled to defeat Iraq, some in the Saudi ruling elite began to talk of creating a Saudi defence force of 200,000 men. This, they argued, would allow the Kingdom to take care of its own defence and thus avoid calling in the assistance of outside powers in a direct and, some argued, humiliating way.[13]

Although this plan captured the imagination of some and appealed to the sense of independence and desire for self-sufficiency of many, it was not a practicable solution. Not only would it require the introduction of general conscription, but it might also create armed forces that could, in time, threaten the very regime that had created it – as in the case of most of the other Middle Eastern states that had rapidly expanded their armed forces.

At the same time, to respond to ideas in the region concerning the importance of 'collective regional security', and to reduce dependence on forces from outside the Arab world, Saudi Arabia, together with the other members of the GCC, Egypt and Syria, signed the Damascus Declaration in March 1991. This declaration envisaged creating a defence pact whereby Egypt and Syria would provide the manpower for a force that would be financed by the Gulf states and stationed in the GCC states to boost the numbers and credibility of their own forces. Building on the cooperation established in the war against Iraq, this was intended to be a 'culturally sensitive' way of organising the defence of Saudi Arabia and the smaller Gulf states.

In fact, this approach proved to be 'culturally sensitive' in more ways than one. The Saudis and others soon realised that the presence of Syrian and Egyptian troops in the Gulf would limit their own ability to determine the priorities in Gulf security. The GCC states were also not prepared to subsidise these forces on the scale expected by the Egyptian and Syrian governments. Finally, if the military threats which these troops were meant to counter were likely to come from Iraq and Iran, then the record of Egypt and Syria, which had taken opposing sides in the Iran–Iraq war, was not a reassuring one.

As a result, Egyptian and Syrian troops were withdrawn in 1991 and the Damascus Declaration lost its viability. It lived on as a forum in which the eight countries could meet from time to time, providing yet another platform from which to express general views relevant to whatever happened to concern them at the time.

However, as far as Saudi Arabia was concerned, the GCC was also an unsuitable vehicle for any effective defence against the military threats represented by either Iraq or Iran. This attitude did not prevent the Saudi government from lending its support to commissions of enquiry within the framework of the GCC aimed at exploring what the implications might be should the Council seek to transform the largely token Peninsular Shield Force into an effective military force. Most notably, this led to the proposal by Oman that, in order to be taken seriously, the GCC would have to create a force of at least 100,000 with a command independent of any of the Council's governments and answerable to the GCC collectively.[14] The implications of this for Saudi dominance within the GCC, as well as for the authority of the Council as an organisation (as opposed to that of the states' rulers) ensured that the plan was shelved.

One of the principal values of the GCC for Saudi Arabia was the 'security cordon' it provided, not so much in terms of military security, but of internal security. Mistrustful of Iran's intentions, as well as of sections of its own population, the Saudi government still fears Iran's capacity to threaten it through subversion and internal political agitation. These suspicions are never far from the surface.

> The Tehran regime ... raises its voice in lamentation and wailing over the loss of trust between Iran and neighbouring states. However, the truth ... is that the regime is planting ill-will, entrenching instability and threatening the region's security by attempting to impose its domination and tutelage on it, although it does not possess anything that may qualify it for that except malice and hatred of life and the living. It is due to all that that no one has or will believe what the senior figures of the regime in Iran say, because their actions disprove their statements.[15]

It was in the light of such fears that the Saudi government organised bilateral security agreements with the GCC states during the 1980s. In 1995, a more comprehensive security agreement, drawn up and promoted at the initiative of Prince Nayef, was signed by all the GCC states except Kuwait and Qatar. Focusing on extradition and the exchange of intelligence information, it was intended to drive home the fact that 'any harm to a signatory state cannot be tolerated in any of the countries [of the GCC]'.[16]

The Saudi government also strengthened its defence cooperation with the US. Close as that cooperation had become, it was clear that the Saudi government wanted to set some limits. This was particularly evident in the aftermath of the 1991 Gulf War, when the US sought a more detailed and extensive formal agreement with Saudi Arabia to supersede the rather general 1977 Military Training Mission Treaty. The US hoped that the new agreement would include, among other things, provision for the prepositioning of sufficient equipment for at least one US division to facilitate future military assistance.

The Saudi government was wary of any such prepositioning agreement before it acquired the arms it wanted from the US. These were included in the massive arms requests submitted to the US in 1991 and 1992. The reluctance of the Saudi ruling elite also had to do with the sensitivity of the issue of housing foreign bases on Saudi soil. The Saudi government was willing to countenance the presence of an estimated 5,000 US service personnel as part of various training and maintenance missions connected with air defence, and with the new weapons systems which Saudi Arabia was acquiring. However, signing a public agreement on prepositioning military materiel which would require a permanent US military presence was something the Saudi government could not bring itself to do.

Instead, it continued to pursue its policy of massive arms purchases. This approach was evident before the 1991 Gulf War, but the experience of those months and the Saudi perception that Iraq and Iran would remain dangers have greatly stimulated it.[17] Since then, Saudi Arabia has placed orders for some $20bn worth of armaments, with heavy emphasis on advanced fighter aircraft, missile-defence systems and main battle tanks. The lion's share of these orders have gone to US contractors, but both the UK and France received substantial contracts. Thus, apart from the military functions and the merits of the equipment purchased, Saudi policy appears to have been aimed at cementing its relations with its Western allies, particularly the US.

It is difficult to say how much of this equipment was purchased with the Iranian threat specifically in mind. Only in one or two cases has it been possible to see a direct response to moves by the Iranians, such as the Saudi purchase of increased quantities of anti-submarine technology when Iran took delivery of its first Russian submarine. The Strategic Missile Force which was initially intended to act as a deterrent, principally against Iranian attack, has become a more general 'deterrent force against all those who attack this holy country and its honourable people', as Prince Sultan put it.[18] Equally, much of the equipment ordered seems to have been geared to the kind of threat which Iraq represented in 1990–91. Nevertheless, efforts by Iran to build its own arsenal during the 1990s were not lost on the Saudi government. Whether in connection with the Iranian attempt to reconstruct its air force and armoured strength, in efforts made to strengthen its naval forces or its alleged determination to acquire a nuclear capability,[19] the Saudi government has tended to believe the worst whilst hoping for the best.

Thus, differences between Iran and Saudi Arabia and the GCC were by no means eliminated with the emergence of the Iraqi threat and Iran's change in attitude. Iran clearly wanted to discourage, weaken and eventually eliminate (or make unnecessary) security ties between these states and outside powers. Iran has agreed not to make an issue of these foreign defence ties and to settle for an agreement to disagree. Yet Iranian propaganda and Tehran's pursuit of regional policies that undermine Saudi Arabia's position have clearly complicated the fostering of trust necessary for building regional security. In addition, Iran's conception of a regional security arrangement involves all the Gulf states, which is not the basis on which Saudi Arabia formed the GCC. Iran perceives *a* or rather *the* leading role for itself, a view rejected by Saudi Arabia because it believes that Iran's wishes would be fundamentally inimical to its own interests. Iran's view of regional security still diverges from that of its principal rival, Saudi Arabia, and its policies have done little to dispel misgivings.

Regional Security

Contrasting views on regional security in Iran and Saudi Arabia derive in part from the diametrically different lessons the two states learned between 1979 and 1991. Whereas Iran has concluded that there can be no regional security without its own participation, Saudi Arabia has concluded that there can be none without outside involvement. Iran's view is that it must include all the littoral states. Clearly a regional arrangement excluding Iran would be pointless. Such an arrangement would also include Iraq eventually (although not while Saddam Hussein remains in power). From the Saudi perspective, however, there is no particular virtue in *regional* security arrangements for their own sake. Saudi Arabia might pay lip-service to such a notion but even in the case of the GCC, the organisation has less to do with the security of the Gulf as a region than with the security of the regimes of its members. By definition, as well as by intention, neither Iraq nor Iran could have any part in this. These contrasting views of regional security, and indeed of the political definition of the region itself, have complicated Iran–Saudi relations over a number of the issues which have involved other Gulf states during the past few years.

Abu Musa in Iran–Saudi Relations

The first incident blocking movement towards *rapprochement* after the new chapter in Iran–GCC relations in 1991 was over the island of Abu Musa. This island and two others (the greater and lesser Tunbs) had been the object of conflicting claims by Iran and the Emirates of Sharjah and Ras Al-Khaimah, constituent members of the UAE since its formation in 1971. The claims, shrouded in history, were dealt with pragmatically as Britain was departing from the Gulf.[20] Iran relinquished its claim to Bahrain in 1970, but insisted on its other claims and annexed the two (uninhabited) Tunb islands. In November 1971, Iran reached an arrangement, or *modus vivendi*, with Sharjah over Abu Musa, in which both parties retained their claim to complete sovereignty, while sharing the administration of the island. Iran was to compensate Sharjah for any oil discovered and exploited. Both states were free to deploy military forces or other elements on its respective designated parts of the island. The agreement withstood the revolution in Iran, the war with Iraq and the claims of states like Libya and Iraq that the islands were Arab territory which Sharjah had no right to relinquish.

In April and August 1992, Iran imposed restrictions on travel to and from the area administered by Sharjah, including the right of UAE nationals to visit and work on the island, allegedly for security reasons. This encroachment on the UAE's rights was taken up very quickly by the GCC and later by the Arab League. Words and recriminations were exchanged and positions hardened. The issue quickly became a yardstick by which the GCC states judged Iranian intentions and the fulcrum on which Arab–Iranian relations were to balance. Encouraged by Arab support, the UAE expanded the issue, linking it to the hitherto dormant issue of the Tunb islands. The Abu Musa affair illustrates the ambiguity of Iranian intentions and the fragility of its relations with the Arab Gulf states and underscores the degree to which the past exercises a continuing influence on present threat and security perceptions.

Iran's motives for intruding on Sharjah's (or the UAE's) rights in 1992 are obscure. There are many possible explanations: it was a probe of the Arab states or of the United States; it exploited Arab weakness; it was a signal of Iran's assertiveness and a warning that it could not be ignored in regional security; it was dictated by military or strategic (i.e., maritime) necessity; or it was the product of domestic political infighting, necessitating a hard line. Iran's action was consistent with most – indeed all – of these explanations.[21]

Iran insists that it has not repudiated its 1971 agreement and has only 'strengthened control and supervision' over the island of Abu Musa. It was not clear whether this was strategic calculation or administrative rigidity, but what is incontrovertible is that Iran misjudged the GCC's response. The sovereignty issue was taken by the Arab states as an indicator of Iran's overall expansionist aims in the Gulf.

Saudi Arabia took the lead in the GCC in condemning Iran and linking Abu Musa with the Tunbs. While Iran believed the issue to be lost in the miasma of Arab politics and atavistic fears, the question of the islands became a key touchstone of Saudi credibility; it was imperative for the Saudis to champion a cause which had suddenly become a major concern to one of the GCC states. Had it failed to do so, or had it sought to downplay the issue, the security compact at the heart of the GCC itself would have been thrown into question, not simply because of the external threat from Iran, but also because of the new internal resonance of such territorial issues in the politics of the UAE.[22]

Furthermore, as far as inter-Arab politics were concerned, it was inevitable that the question of the Tunbs should have been raised as soon as the issue of Abu Musa was discussed. This 'shameful surrender of Arab land' had been vehemently condemned in 1971 when Saudi Arabia and other littoral states were accused by some Arab states of bowing to pressure from the imperialists, in collusion with Iran, and turning a blind eye to Iran's seizure of these islands. In 1992, Iraq and other states hostile to Saudi Arabia began to home in on the issue of the Tunbs again, publicly proclaiming the 'need' for Arabs to reassert their rights. Domestically and regionally, therefore, whatever the feelings of the Saudi government itself, it would have been impossible to support Sharjah on the question of Abu Musa without raising Ras Al-Khaimah's claim to the Tunbs. Consequently, the Saudis insisted that the islands belonged to the UAE and called on Iran 'to prove its sincere intentions' and to settle the matter peacefully, to 'return' the islands to the UAE and to respect standards and conventions based 'on mutual respect and non-interference in the domestic affairs of states' as a precondition for 'constructive cooperation'.[23]

As Iran saw it, the Saudis were seeking the relinquishment of *any* Iranian claim, not only to Abu Musa, but also to the Tunbs, implying a return not to the status quo in March 1992, but to the situation before November 1971. The dispute, which Iran calls a 'misunderstanding', thus obstructed normal relations. Of course, the fact that a member of the Ras Al-Khaimah ruling family, Sheikh Fahim Bin Sultan Al-Qasimi, was the new, Saudi-backed Secretary-General of the GCC ensured a high profile for this disagreement. Echoing language used to describe the other long-running Arab cause – the question of 'occupied Palestine' – Al-Qasimi, in one of his first public interviews, lamented the fact that 'Iran has not taken any initiative showing it intends to withdraw from the three occupied islands. This does not help stability in the region'.[24] This theme was later taken up at the meeting of GCC foreign ministers in Riyadh in October 1994, where Iran was roundly condemned for laying down 'unacceptable conditions' for resuming talks on the islands.[25]

For the GCC states, Iran's behaviour called into question all of its commitments to sovereignty and territorial integrity. This was reiterated at the Council summit meeting of December 1993 and was clearly expressed by its Secretary-General in 1994 when he was asked about the 'foundations and criteria for the establishment of good relations with Iran'. He replied, 'At present, these foundations are non-existent because there is a real Iranian occupation. The occupation must end, then we can talk about normal relations between Iran and the Gulf states ... We are interested in establishing good relations with it [Iran], but occupation prevents that'.[26]

In 1995, the GCC, in its ministerial sessions, castigated Iran for its lack of progress on the issue. The UAE Deputy Prime Minister, Sheikh Sultan, characterised Iran's occupation of the islands as posing a direct regional threat.[27] In an effort to bring about a measure of mutual understanding in this highly charged atmosphere, the government of Qatar brought together Iranian and UAE delegations in Doha in November 1995 to discuss the issue. These relatively junior delegations were supposed to draw up an agenda for a later meeting of more senior figures on both sides. However, after five days of discussion no agreement was forthcoming, and the talks ended inconclusively. Despite this inauspicious start, Iran, which has always claimed that this matter should be settled bilaterally between itself and the UAE, tried to maintain momentum by suggesting that there should be a further round of talks in Tehran.[28] There was no response from the UAE. Instead, in a move guaranteed to annoy Iran, the GCC summit of early December condemned Iran for its intransigence.[29] This was followed soon after by a statement supporting the UAE and its claims to Abu Musa and the Tunbs at a meeting of the foreign ministers of the eight Arab Damascus Declaration states.

To Iran, the dispute over the islands is more symbolic and political than territorial or legal. Iran sees the issue not in terms of its relations with the GCC, but as part of its jousting with the United States. Iran's action over the islands might be seen as a *response* to Washington's refusal to take into account its interests or to 'include' it in a regional arrangement. Moreover, as Iran sees it, the nature of regional politics is weighted against it whenever it has a difference with an Arab state. Of the plethora of territorial disputes in the region, only this one was inflated into a region-wide issue and imbued with symbolic importance.[30] The tendency to 'Arabise' issues, wrapping them in the mantle of Arab nationalism and patrimony, raises the stakes, making a resolution more difficult. Iran experienced this with Iraq on the long-running territorial dispute over the Shatt Al-Arab waterway, on the islands in 1971 and now again after 1992.

Iran adamantly refuses to accept the 'Arabisation' of the dispute and condemns Saudi Arabia for 'interfering'.[31] Tehran insists that the issue is a bilateral one that can be settled by direct negotiations, without preconditions or linkages (e.g., to the ownership of the Tunbs). It therefore rejects any 'internationalisation' of the dispute and involvement by the International Court of Justice (ICJ).[32] Furthermore, it points out that the GCC, 'rather than resort to commotion' which results only in the 'aggravation of difficulties', should encourage a bilateral settlement and then focus on Israel's behaviour instead of being diverted by mythical stories about the Iranian threat.[33]

By contrast, the failure of the 1993 bilateral negotiations between Iran and the UAE led the GCC states to decide that the matter should go to the ICJ. This is now the position not only of the GCC states, but also of the Arab League and the Damascus Declaration states. (Saudi Arabia has sought to avoid responsibility for taking unilateral action on the issue.) Whether or not the UAE has a strong case to put before the ICJ is immaterial; as far as the Saudi government is concerned, this way of resolving the dispute has an Arab consensus. Whatever the outcome of the case (if it ever gets to court), the judgement will be accepted and Saudi Arabia and the other GCC states cannot be accused of 'betrayal' – except perhaps by the present Iraqi government whose view of the legitimacy of international institutions is similar in some ways to that of Iran.

Saudi Arabia's attempted use of Syria as a mediator appears to have failed and, indeed, Syria's subscription to the general 'Arab' interpretation of the dispute cannot have boosted its reputation with Iran as a neutral mediator.[34] Nor was the Iranian Foreign Minister any more successful in persuading the UAE to open restricted bilateral talks as Iran preferred.[35]

Domestically, the island(s) issue has become a politically charged one in Iran, insofar as the regime cannot be seen to give up territory inherited from monarchical Iran. This is a matter of nationalism rather than ideology.[36] The more publicity it has received, and the more the Arab states have insisted on the return of the islands, the more it has become a test of resolve and determination. Inexorably, given the nature of domestic politics and pressures at work in both Iran and the GCC states, especially Saudi Arabia, their governments' positions have hardened. In 1992, President Rafsanjani, who had sought to play down the crisis, became exasperated with Arab reaction and warned that anyone attempting to reach the islands would have to go through a 'sea of blood'. The threat was later repeated and re-emphasised.[37]

This threat, in turn, provoked a sharp Saudi response. Such language and such an attitude is seen in Saudi Arabia as symptomatic of Iran's inner political crises, and thus part of the radical and interventionist impulses that make Iran an unsettling neighbour.[38] Furthermore, the images used by the Arab side summon attitudes long associated in the Arab world with the 'occupation of Palestine', raising fears that the issue may become as symbolically and politically charged, thereby complicating any attempt to resolve it by peaceful means.

Bahrain in Iran–Saudi Relations
Political disturbances in the state of Bahrain since 1994 have given rise to accusations of Iranian involvement. In light of Iran's efforts to 'export' its revolution to the island in 1982–83, and the fact that uniquely among the Gulf emirates Bahrain has a majority Shi'i population, such suspicions are reasonable, especially as Bahrain enjoys close relations with Saudi Arabia. It has concluded a defence agreement with the United States and hosts a US naval facility. For these reasons it would be considered an important or likely objective for destabilisation. Bahrain's social composition would also make it vulnerable; its Shi'i majority, insofar as they are ruled by a Sunni family and an authoritarian system of government, fall into the category of 'oppressed', as sections of the Iranian media and some official circles have made plain.

It is difficult to determine how much the disturbances in Bahrain have been purely the result of domestic forces, and how much has been due to encouragement from Iranian sympathisers. Iran no doubt stands to benefit from any anti-US movements; it also has an interest in seeing the GCC split and Saudi Arabia distracted. Improving the lot of the oppressed – and especially the Shi'a – is a central plank in its revolutionary policies. In the past, links between Qom and clerics in other countries have been used to foment, encourage and possibly even direct political agitation. In Bahrain, Shi'i mosques and prayer leaders have been important catalysts in the disturbances. However, the centrality of the religious network is a characteristic feature of any Shi'i community and is not evidence in itself of Iranian government direction.

Iran has depicted the protests in Bahrain as domestic in origin, motivated by the demand for political reform and as such applicable to all the GCC states. Its radio interviews of opposition figures reflect these themes;[39] one observed that, despite the wide social support for the protests encompassing secularists, technocrats and Islamists, the Bahrain government emphasised the Sunni/Shi'i divisions in the disturbances 'to gain the sympathy of Western governments, by giving the impression that we are controlled by Iran'.[40]

Iran reacted sharply to a statement by the Saudi Interior Minister which claimed that foreign hands were behind Bahrain's turmoil. Iranian radio insisted that Saudi Arabia sought to harm Iran's relations with Bahrain, to divide Iran and the GCC and to exercise a leadership role.[41] For the Saudi government, the developments in Bahrain are clearly worrying, whether they are orchestrated by Iran or are the result of Bahraini politics. If the latter, the themes of constitutionalism, free association and organisation or of communal reaction against sectarian discrimination are ones which the Saudi authorities have no desire to see spread to their own country, particularly in view of the proximity of the Eastern Province to Bahrain. In this province, the history of workers' organisations in the oil industry and the pattern of communal unrest among Shi'a contain a number of parallels with similar developments in Bahrain, and Saudi authorities have attempted over the past few years to ensure that no such eruption should recur on its territory.

The events in Bahrain have served as a reminder of forces which may lie just beneath the surface in Saudi Arabia itself. Under these circumstances it is not surprising that the Saudi authorities have publicly subscribed to Bahrain's allegations of Iranian involvement. In part, this may have much to do with the solidarity of the Gulf rulers and their general unwillingness to admit that unrest within their kingdoms may have domestic causes, for which they themselves must shoulder responsibility. Saudi Arabia is as keen as any to maintain the fiction that political opposition is largely the work of external enemies, as well as to display solidarity with its regional allies, including the ruling Al-Khalifah of Bahrain. At the same time, Saudi Arabia may genuinely fear Iran's ability to strike a sympathetic chord in the populations of Arab Shi'a living on the western side of the Gulf. Even if this Iranian involvement is only verbal – using such language as the 'exploitation of the oppressed' and encouraging Shi'i resentment of Sunni domination or discrimination – it may have the potential to mobilise disaffected elements in Saudi Arabia itself.

The inability of the Bahraini government to end the protests, whether by concessions or by force, led to renewed violence during 1995 and to reports that Saudi troops were involved in maintaining order.[42] In early 1996, the Bahraini government arrested eight prominent Shi'a and openly accused a 'foreign government' (a code phrase for Iran) of directing specific acts of sabotage.[43] Apart from Qatar, the rest of the GCC seemed to share this interpretation. In emphasising the issue of the Shi'a specifically, these states remained anxious that unrest might spread among their own Shi'i populations. Furthermore, insofar as opposition demands centred on political reform – including the restoration of the Constitution and more repesentative institutions, such as national assemblies – these demands were seen as a threat to the current order prevailing in Gulf politics. The GCC states, led by Saudi Arabia, were thus disposed to treat the disturbances in Bahrain as a 'conspiracy' and a threat to regional security, blaming Iran.[44] In early June 1996, Bahrain withdrew its ambassador from Tehran and for the first time directly accused Iran of funding and supporting a campaign of subversion.

The issue of Iran's role is linked to other considerations – the degree to which existing social discontent is ripe for 'manipulation', and the extent of that discontent in encompassing other social groups besides Shi'a or Bahrainis of Iranian descent. While there is some evidence of verbal Iranian encouragement for the opposition movement in Bahrain, there is little to suggest that Iran plays a central role. The breadth of the movement encompassing Sunnis, democrats and professional classes belies such an interpretation.[45] In the final analysis, Iran's role can hardly be considered central to Bahrain's problems. Yet this does not change the reality of Bahrain's perception that it remains vulnerable to destabilisation by its Iranian neighbour, nor do such perceptions reduce the limitations this puts on even genuine efforts by Iran to improve its relations with the Arab states of the Persian Gulf. Iran is thus a pretext for avoiding political reform and a catalyst for maintaining intra-Arab cohesion in the face of a common threat.

The Inter-Arab Disputes: Qatar and Yemen

Iran sees Saudi Arabia as being behind its problems with the GCC. Saudi Arabia, as the leading GCC state, can use that organisation to promote its own interests. Reflecting the official view in Tehran, Iranian scholars tirelessly point to the fact that the GCC is a vehicle for Saudi dominance, that the Saudis use the 'Iranian threat' to strengthen their position, and that the Kingdom was built on an expansionism which it has still not renounced.[46] Given this Saudi dominance, Iran's policy is to weaken the Council by aggravating its internal differences, but without posing a direct threat to it. It does so by emphasising disputes within the GCC, cultivating bilateral relations with individual members and underscoring the Council's inability to meet its members needs.

Iran's reaction to the Qatar–Saudi border dispute and its position on Yemen illustrate its desire to weaken the GCC. During a border incident between Saudi Arabia and Qatar in 1992, the same year as the revival of the Abu Musa dispute, Iran made sympathetic noises towards Qatar. Reportedly, it offered to conclude a joint defence treaty with it and to supply 30,000 soldiers.[47] Although this offer was not pursued, Iran has since cultivated a special relationship with Qatar, including cooperation in supplying fresh water. Iranian officials point to relations with Qatar as a model for bilateral relations with other sheikhdoms.[48] Despite the potential for differences between the two states (e.g., on overlapping claims to gas fields located near Qatar), the relationship suits them both. Iran welcomed the in-house *coup d'état* in Qatar in June 1995, expecting that state to continue its independent policy.

For Iran, the relationship is an opportunity to show the smaller littoral states the utility of offsetting Saudi power and Arabian peninsula dominance with balanced relations with the power across the Gulf. Inevitably, Iran's capacity and intention to 'increase its influence and intervention in regional squabbles' has caused concern in Saudi Arabia, where there is a clear notion of the proper zone of Saudi influence – and a proprietary idea of the local 'squabbles', especially those which involve Saudi Arabia itself.[49]

Given the possible number of boundary disputes between Saudi Arabia and its neighbours, or between members of the GCC, the potential for disaffection is considerable. In light of the growing Saudi–Qatari dispute towards the end of 1994, and Qatar's refusal even to attend the GCC's Interior Ministers' meeting that year to discuss an important security agreement, Qatar's disaffection was worrying. It was scarcely surprising, then, that the Saudi media reacted sharply to Iran's exploitation of this dispute, attacking the Iranian regime for 'searching for any superficial, emergent dispute within the Gulf Cooperation Council in an attempt to disturb the fraternal relations existing between the GCC states and ignite differences between them'.[50] Saudi anger and anxiety at the refusal of not only Qatar but also Kuwait to sign the security agreement cannot have been allayed by the Iranian commentary which referred to 'the differences between the (Persian) GCC member states on the joint security agreement', and the 'deep rift among members'.[51]

Iran took a similar line against Saudi Arabia as the Yemen civil war erupted in 1994. Iran saw GCC policy as being based on the traditional idea of keeping Yemen weak, hence the Saudis' encouragement in 1994 of the south's secession from the union. Iranian officials and commentaries castigated Saudi 'interference' as 'aggravating' the issue and serving US interests.[52]

For the Saudi government, the defeat of the Aden secessionists was a setback. However, given the nature of the Saudi–Yemen relationship, it was unlikely to be a lasting obstacle to Saudi influence in Yemen, whether directly on the government in Sana'a or through the various tribal and political factions. Nor was there much that Iran could do to alter this peculiarly intimate relationship. Nevertheless, Iran's willingness to use Saudi–Yemeni tensions to taunt Saudi Arabia led to a predictably sharp response.

> The Iranian mullahs [are] using their inspired evil capabilities to deceive, destroy and fish in the waters that they work toward dirtying in the same manner as the trumpets of their media have attempted over the past two days to kindle the flames of sedition between the kingdom and its sister, the Republic of Yemen – after the mullahs noticed the occurrence of a small misunderstanding over the issue of the Saudi–Yemeni border. But this has not achieved the wicked desires in engineering bloody confrontations between the sisterly Arab countries that they were seeking.[53]

The subsequent agreement between Saudi Arabia and Yemen regulating their border differences required the end of assistance to opposition elements in each other's countries, 'which' (Iranian radio gloated) 'is tantamount to a retreat on the part of Riyadh'.[54] In fact, this agreement was testimony more to Saudi Arabia's power and Yemen's economic prostration than to the thwarting of Riyadh's ambitions.

Iran's willingness to exploit its rival's differences with its neighbours contains an element of 'tit-for-tat'. In the midst of the sometimes strident Saudi emphasis on the 'threat' from Iran (and Iraq), pointing out Saudi difficulties is a healthy corrective. Iran has some basis for exploiting suspicion of Saudi power among the smaller states. At the very least, Iran can offer bilateral ties to mitigate the existence of the GCC. But such ties will not be the basis for an alternative regional security scheme. Indeed, in the case both of intra-GCC disputes and of Yemen, the main effect of Iran's efforts appears to have been to worsen its own relationship with Saudi Arabia.

Neither Qatar nor Yemen, for all their differences with the Saudi government, can afford to ignore Saudi Arabia or, indeed, to alienate it in any fundamental sense. Qatari disaffection has shown itself on a number of occasions, most dramatically when the ruler of Qatar, Sheikh Hamid Bin Khalifah Al-Thani walked out of the GCC summit in Oman in December 1995, ostensibly to protest the manner in which a Saudi, Jamil Al-Hujaylan, was chosen as the next Secretary-General of the GCC.[55] By mid-1996, the Qatari ruler was indicating that he understood the limits of Qatar's leverage over Saudi Arabia. Thus, Iranian involvement with Qatar and Yemen has merely confirmed the basic Saudi mistrust of Iran's intentions, without yielding anything very positive by way of return for Iran itself.

Iraq in Iran–Saudi Relations

Distrust is the common element in the triangular relations among the three major Persian Gulf states. None trusts the other and each seeks to widen its area of influence and enhance its leverage against the others. With Iraq practically 'excluded' from Gulf politics since 1991, Iran's rivalry with Saudi Arabia has been more direct. Iran has used the threat of a reconciliation with Iraq to increase its leverage with the GCC and the United States. Whether it is in Iran's interest to be equated with Iraq is another question. How real the 'Iraqi option' is, and how much Iran will retain control over it, are also uncertain.

Iran has certain potentially overlapping interests with Iraq, but these are not weighty enough to dictate a decisive opening to Baghdad. Divergences are at least as significant as areas of common interest. An additional consideration is Iran's relationship with Syria which may be strained if Iran collaborates too closely with Iraq. Furthermore, if overlapping interests are a consideration, Iran may have many, if not more, in common with Saudi Arabia. A policy of equidistance between Iraq and Saudi Arabia might give Iran more options than an alliance with Baghdad. Opening up to Iraq in any case is not without risks. It may increase Iraq's leverage and give it new options, perhaps leading eventually to an Iraqi–Saudi *rapprochement*. For example, Iraq might seek to exploit the insecurity of the GCC states *vis-à-vis* Iran by reviving its role as 'defender of the Arab East'. This is a noticeable theme in recent Iraqi commentaries.[56] Hence Iran risks a renewed polarisation of the Gulf on Arab–Persian lines.

Iran's diplomacy towards Iraq is an uncertain venture; tilting towards Iraq promises increased leverage, but at the risk of diminishing Iran's current influence which has been achieved by Iraq's enforced absence. Iran sees Iraq as an asset in its difficulties with the US. Less clear is how Iran views Iraq in terms of Persian Gulf politics, and how it sees the presence or absence of that state affecting Iran's position with the other Gulf states. The lack of clarity stems from the gap between Iran's declared policy and its actual interests and from Tehran's tendency to react tactically rather than to plan strategically.

Iran and Saudi Arabia both want a weakened, though intact, Iraq. This has enabled the two states to follow parallel policies in supporting Iraq's territorial integrity and backing Iraqi opposition forces[57]. Both Iran and Saudi Arabia have reason to feel threatened by a militarily strong Iraq, which would be a potential threat to each of them that neither poses, in the same way, to the other. However bitter the relationship and intense the rivalry, the prospect of full-scale military operations between Iran and Saudi Arabia remains remote in a way that it does not between each of them and Iraq. (True, this is largely due to geography. But the two states are politically different from Iraq and their relationship reflects it.) A weak Iraq intensifies Iran–Saudi rivalry; a revived or stronger Iraq would moderate it, while complicating the balance for both parties.

However, as far as the Saudi government is concerned, a strengthened Iraq cannot be contemplated as long as Saddam Hussein remains in office. His 'betrayal' in 1990 remains keenly felt. Quite apart from the vituperation which followed as Saddam denounced Saudi leaders for inviting the US into the Kingdom, it was the sense of personal betrayal and breach of faith which appeared to rankle the Saudis. It is difficult to see Saddam Hussein successfully rehabilitating himself, having broken all the codes of Gulf politics. For this reason, Saddam himself has been the frequent target of vehement denunciation by the Saudi media, although Saudi officials have generally been more circumspect.[58]

Nevertheless, Saddam's political survival has clearly been of great concern to Saudi Arabia – as it has to some of the other Gulf states – in a number of contradictory ways. It both contains the prospects of revanchism and takes Iraq out of the 'game' of Gulf politics, in the sense of denying the Saudis the opportunity to counterbalance Iran with the Iraqi link. On one level, this has encouraged the Saudi strategies of unilateral defence procurement and of drawing ever closer to the US. On another level, it has led the Saudis to entertain thoughts of encouraging the overthrow of Saddam Hussein's regime. To this end, they have encouraged and possibly subsidised a number of Iraqi opposition groups. The early beneficiaries of this attention were disgruntled Iraqi army officers in exile whom the Saudis would dearly love to see in power in Iraq, presiding over a reassuringly Sunni Arab-dominated authoritarian regime.

However, it became increasingly apparent that the chances of such figures ever being able to organise effective opposition, let alone overthrow the present regime, were very small. As a result, in 1992 Saudi Arabia started to cultivate the broad and disparate coalition of the Iraqi National Congress (INC). The significance of this move was not simply that the INC contained representatives of a wide spectrum of Iraqi political opinion, few of whom could be said to be 'natural' allies of a regime such as Saudi Arabia, but also that it gave Saudi authorities contacts with such people as Baqir Al-Hakim. A Shi'i cleric, Al-Hakim heads the Supreme Assembly of Islamic Revolution in Iraq (SAIRI), a group drawn from Iraq's Shi'i community which has its main office in Tehran and has been Iran's principal client in the INC.[59] Given Saddam's resilience, the INC has been no more successful than anyone else in engineering his downfall.

In the meantime, the Saudi government was willing to support UN sanctions against Iraq whilst at the same time urging Iraq to discharge all its obligations under the terms of the UN resolutions. It managed to bring the GCC along with it, although some members, such as Kuwait, needed no persuading. Others, however, particularly those geographically removed from Iraq who were not militarily threatened by it or who wished to act counter to the dominant Saudis, demonstrated their anxiety about the effects of sanctions on Iraq.

So pronounced was this dissent by 1994, particularly by Qatar and Oman, that the Saudi Foreign Minister felt it was time to bring them back into line by re-emphasising the Iraqi danger and the dangers of disunity.

> The Iraqi regime continues to pose a threat to the security and stability of our countries. There are also threats aimed at destroying our cooperation council which represented the solid rock that quashed Iraq's ambitions and thwarted its ugly aggression ... Iraq's latest efforts are ... an attempt to help lift the embargo ... and its attempt to re-establish relations without

respecting and fully implementing these [UN] resolutions and recommendations. It is absolutely crucial to issue resolutions that stress and underline our determined and strong stance regarding this matter, to close the door in the face of any such attempt.[60]

As it transpired, Saudi Arabia had little difficulty keeping the GCC members in line because of Iraq's actions in Kuwait in 1990 and its threatening language which suggested that an unrepentant Saddam Hussein was simply awaiting his opportunity to strike against the Gulf rulers. These events, whatever Iraq's real intention, were used by the Saudi Foreign Minister to draw attention to the 'aggressive intentions it harboured against the fraternal state of Kuwait and all of the Gulf region'.[61] Nevertheless, after official Iraqi recognition of Kuwait following this curious episode, some in the GCC apparently suggested that the Iraqi regime had fulfilled the major conditions for its reintegration into the community of Arab states and that sanctions could be lifted.[62]

It is primarily the small GCC states that have questioned the wisdom and desirability of continued sanctions against Iraq. However, despite its re-established links with Qatar and Oman there has been little suggestion that a close relationship can be contemplated with Iraq under its present political regime. There has been no visible dissent within the ruling Saudi family to its continued hardline policy towards Saddam's Iraq, even when US planes used the Saudi airfield at Dahran to attack Iraqi missile installations in 1993. Consequently, there has been little incentive for the Saudi government to alter its approach to Iraq.

Indeed, it could be said to be an integral part of the strategy the Saudis have adopted with regard to the US. Not only does the existence of an Iraqi military threat continue to excite US policy-makers, but it also underlines the importance of the continued US military commitment to protect Saudi Arabia. This has two beneficial consequences for the Saudi regime. First, it allows Saudi Arabia to order the advanced weapons systems which it might otherwise have had difficulty in acquiring. In the context of past and future Iraqi aggression, Saudi Arabia was and will appear as the 'steadfast ally' of the US, deserving of the full range of arms that the US can supply. Second, the blatant military threat represented by Iraq reinforces US determination to organise the military defence of the Saudi oilfields, and thus of the Kingdom. This strong commitment to Saudi defence is, of course, not simply a deterrent to Iraq, but also to any other state that might be inclined to endanger Saudi Arabia's military security.

What does Iran want from an opening to Iraq? It wants to give the *impression* of an opening. This may increase its leverage with the United States, which may fear an alliance of 'rogue' states, and with the GCC states, which may consider Iran 'the lesser evil'. Such a move would also show Iran that the country is not beleaguered or without choices, that it can take the initiative and surprise its adversaries. The basis for Iran–Iraq cooperation is their reputation as awkward, dangerous and untrustworthy states, which has led to their virtual international isolation. They share hostility towards the United States and an antipathy for the GCC and Saudi Arabia's leadership pretensions, and they both oppose the Arab–Israeli peace process.[63]

However, Iran and Iraq differ on their respective roles in the Gulf, in terms of their relations with the other states of the region and a host of bilateral issues, as well as the immediate issue of Iraq's return to the oil market. The distrust between Iran and Iraq is greater than that between Iran and Saudi Arabia, and is matched only by that between Iraq and Saudi Arabia. This would suggest that the basis for Iran–Saudi cooperation is firmer than that between Tehran and Baghdad. However, this ignores the pressures of the moment on Iran to react to the current US 'Cold War' by demonstrating that it has options, including 'opportunistic alliances'.[64]

Iran has conducted policy towards Iraq on two levels. On one it has sought reconciliation; on the other, it has continued its competition and hardheaded pursuit of its own interests. During *Operation Desert Storm*, Iran was unhappy with the prospect of an isolated, weakened Iraq which would have left the US in a position to decide the future security of the Persian Gulf. Iran tried to arrange a negotiated end to the conflict before the air-phase began in mid-January 1991. In March, President Rafsanjani denounced Saddam Hussein and called on him to resign. Iran's position was that, with a different government, Iraq should participate in a regional security arrangement.[65] Iran, however, denounced subsequent US attacks on Iraq in January 1993 as 'disgraceful'.[66]

From 1993 the pace towards normalisation quickened. In March 1993, Iranian Foreign Minister Ali Akbar Vellayati called for improved relations with Iraq and in May (before the label 'dual containment' was formulated) he announced that steps toward political negotiations, with exchange visits, would soon begin.[67] In June 1993, Iran again condemned a US attack on Iraq as being against the UN Charter.[68] From 1993 onwards there were reports of Iran informally assisting Iraq in breaking the UN embargo and in selling its oil.[69] In February 1994 an Iraqi delegation visited Iran, but further exchanges were halted after a bomb exploded at the holy site of Mashad killing a number of pilgrims. Iran accused Baghdad of complicity because of its support for the opposition Mujahedin forces who were accused of the bombing. In September Iran called for an end to the embargo on Iraq, saying that the country had a vital role to play and that it would be in Iran's 'strategic interest'.[70]

Iran's relations with the US deteriorated even further when Washington announced a total trade embargo in spring 1995. An Iranian Foreign Ministry delegation returned a visit to Baghdad in May. Iranian media now openly referred to the 'common enemy' – the US – as the basis for cooperation between the two countries.[71] Iranian officials were at pains to point out to the Gulf states that any reconciliation between the two countries would not be at the expense of Iran's ties with the Arab Gulf states, stressing that its main purpose was *vis-à-vis* the United States.[72] By July 1995 there was talk of a visit to Baghdad by Vellayati. However, before any real improvement in relations could be expected, substantive progress (i.e., in Iran's view, Iraqi concessions) had to be made on a range of bilateral issues.[73] In September 1995 an Iraqi delegation led by a deputy foreign minister visited Iran. Talks included such topics as the fate of prisoners of war (POWs) (of which some 30,000 allegedly remain in Iran) and those missing in action (MIAs), and working groups were established to tackle these and topics related to the full implementation of UN Security Council Resolution 598 (passed to facilitate the end of the Iran–Iraq War). In 1996, a series of meetings was initiated between Iranian and Iraqi delegations on their common frontier to discuss problems arising from their eight-year war (primarily concerning POWs and MIAs) and thus to pave the way for the 'normalisation' of relations.[74]

On another level, Iranian policy has been tough. Repeatedly (every year since 1991 and often twice or more) Iran has struck militarily at the Mujahedin's bases in eastern Iraq. This is an area where Iran has consistently resorted to force, including air and missile attacks and ground incursions. In addition, since 1993, Iran has launched a series of attacks on forces of the Kurdish Democratic Party (KDP) of Iran based in Iraqi Kurdistan. Iran has justified these as hot pursuit, and as deterrent measures to stop terrorism; Iraq, however, has 'strongly warned' against continued 'flagrant aggression'.[75] Iran postponed discussions for almost a year after it suspected Iraq of complicity in terrorist actions on its territory. It then insisted that a prime condition (*inter alia*) for normalisation would be the expulsion of the Mujahedin from Iraq.[76] At the same time it has given no indication that it will drop support for SAIRI.[77]

How receptive has Iraq been to the possibility of breaking out of its isolation? Less than might be expected. The animosity between it and its neighbour seems to weigh more heavily in Baghdad, probably because the Iraqi leadership suspects Iran's motives. Iraq's policy has thus been poised between offering a 'strategic accord' to Iran and seeking to play the 'balancer' to Iran for the GCC and the West. Before its invasion of Kuwait, Iraq had offered such an accord to Iran.[78] After its defeat, Iraq volunteered to play the role of protector against the Iranian 'threat'.[79] Since then, the Iraqi media, with diminishing hope, have continued to emphasise that all the Arab states should work to lift the embargo, 'because Iraq is an effective and basic Arab Gulf state whose strength has a role in achieving Gulf security and stability' (and so that Iraqis) 'can resume their pan-Arab role'.[80] Iraq condemned the GCC for under-reacting on the Abu Musa dispute with Iran.[81]

Iraq's suspicions about Iran have been voiced by Saddam Hussein; 'the rulers of Iran only resort to deception and lies'. In referring to the Shi'i uprising in Iraq in 1991, he later said it was 'part of the scheme of aggression in which the Iranian rulers played their known role in the chapter of treachery and treason'.[82] Saddam Hussein has not forsaken the Arab card, recalling the Iraqi Army's valiant role 'in defending Iraq and Arabism against the racist anti-Arab expansion that came from the east for eight fierce years'. He depicts the war with Iran in terms of 'the anti-Arab grudge coming from Iran'.[83] In 1995, Saddam again referred to the 'fanatic, deranged minds' of Iranians in the Iran–Iraq War, while offering to cooperate with Iran if it returned the aircraft which Iraq had 'deposited with them' in 1991 and claimed by Iraq to number 148.[84]

The Iraqi media reflect Saddam's ambivalence and distrust, calling for normalisation if Iran is 'sincere' while questioning its motives. 'We are also aware of the hypocritical and opportunist nature of the clerical regime'.[85] In autumn 1995, the Iraqi media began to promote confidence-building between the two countries. They argued that Iran–Iraq cooperation could either be based on substantive 'strategic cooper-ation', or on tactical agreement which in time could acheive the same result. In either case, the media argued, the result would be the same. 'The regional balance of power will begin to change, not to the interest of the United States and its satellites, who will be quite reluctant to antagonise both Iraq and Iran'.[86] Tariq Aziz, while trying to convince others again of the need to (re-)constitute Iraq as the guardian of the Arabs' eastern flank, also insisted that Iraq sought good relations with Iran and complained that Iran did not reciprocate.[87] Iranians, in turn, remained sceptical about Iraqi intentions.[88]

Most recently, Iraq's suspicions of Iranian intentions have been sharpened by Iran's tendency to involve itself in the continuing turmoil of the Kurdish zone of northern Iraq. Initially Iran had been, for understandable ideological reasons, a supporter of the main Kurdish Islamist party. In the internecine struggles among the Iraqi Kurds that erupted during 1994 and 1995, the Islamist party was allied with Massoud Barzani's KDP against Jalal Talabani's Popular Union of Kurdistan (PUK). However, at the time the Iranian government believed that it stood to gain influence by acting as a mediator between the warring factions. This was due to the inability of both the INC (with which Iran and the Iraqi groups it supports were becoming increasingly disillusioned) and others to mediate effectively between the Kurdish factions. In particular, it seems that Iran believed that if it could play a role in bringing the Kurds together it would preclude reassertion of direct control over the zone and would simultaneously reduce the influence of the United States.

With the apparent failure of US attempts at mediation between the KDP and the PUK in Ireland in summer 1995, Iran stepped in. KDP and PUK delegations made their way to Tehran in October 1995 and an agreement of sorts was hammered out. This modest success paved the way for a large delegation of Iranian officials to visit the Iraqi Kurdish zone at the end of the year. However, this involvement led to increasing Iranian support for the PUK during 1996. Naturally, these activities did not go unnoticed. The Iraqi media launched a fierce attack on Iran warning of the dire consequences of continued Iranian intervention.[89] Nevertheless, these fulminations neither halted Iranian involvement in Kurdistan nor lessened the Iraqi desire to resolve some of its other outstanding differences with Iran. As a consequence, at the very time that Iraqi and Iranian delegations were meeting to discuss these issues and rumours were circulating about a Vellayati visit to Baghdad, Iraqi Kurdish groups continued to visit Tehran to ask for Iranian mediation.[90] This has provoked sharp criticism from Iraq, where the official press denounced Iran as pursuing an 'unscrupulous' policy towards Iraq and of interfering in its neighbour's internal affairs.[91]

An additional and critical question is whether Iran's strategic interests in the Persian Gulf are served by Iraq's 'return' to regional politics. It could be argued that a weak, isolated Iraq serves Iran better; it enhances Iran's role in the Gulf, it poses no military threat and, if excluded from the oil market it allows a revenue-hungry Iran to sell more oil. A revived Iraq in alliance with Iran would certainly challenge the United States, but in the process it would reduce Iran's weight in the Gulf and gravely complicate the oil market, which would have to adapt to Iraq's need to sell (more rather than less) oil.

Above all, if Iran engineered an 'alliance' with Iraq, how would that fit in with its other Gulf interests – influence over Saudi Arabia and the GCC, an increased regional role, and the reduction or elimination of the US presence and influence in the region? Iran would run the risk of both driving the GCC closer together and, under the Saudi wing, closer to the US, as well as justifying the US presence in the region. In brief, the 'Iraqi card' holds risks as well as opportunities for Iranian diplomacy. It may be more effective as an implicit threat than as a serious strategy.

Barriers to Rapprochement – *A Conclusion*
A number of basic 'structural factors' have tended to complicate Iran's relations with the Arab Gulf states and specifically with Saudi Arabia. Geopolitical elements, such as disparities in power, in population size, strategic depth, coastline and other asymmetries, in part capture the idea; so, too, does reference to the Gulf – whose very nomenclature is disputed – as illustrative of an Arab–Persian divide, cultural and historical as well as geopolitical. There is also a sectarian component in that Iran is the only Shi'i state and most of the world's Shi'a live in an arc around the shores of the Persian Gulf. This has increased the Arab rulers' sense of vulnerability and has made harmonious relations with Tehran difficult.

These basic factors have been exacerbated by the conduct of the Islamic republic. In seeking a leadership role, initially by exporting the revolution, and later by diplomatic means and through appeals to Islamic solidarity, Tehran has ensured that relations remain infused with suspicion. The Arab states fear that significant parts of their populations may be manipulated by an unfriendly power. The very susceptibility of these sectors to such appeals, reflecting their poor integration and lack of representative institutions, increases the fury and suspicion of the Arab authorities, yet allows political agitation to be attributed to foreign designs rather than to indigenous discontent.

Regionally, the Saudi government has invoked foreign threats to ensure its leadership of, and promote cohesion within, the GCC.[92] Saudi

Arabia can play upon the GCC states' anxieties and attribute all the area's problems to Iran (and Iraq). This is easy enough, as noted in the domestic disturbances in Bahrain. In cases where Iran has a bilateral dispute with a neighbour, as with the UAE, Saudi Arabia can make the issue a test-case of Iran's intentions, freezing relations until it is suitably resolved. Although not all of the Gulf rulers are willing to subscribe to the Saudi view to the same degree and may seek to establish their independence by cultivating closer relations with Iran, there are limits in this regard.

This state of affairs favours Saudi Arabia's extension of its authority in the peninsula and handicaps Iran, which is obliged to prove its good intentions repeatedly. Riyadh has sought to depict Iran as an irresponsible menace; in this it has had much help from Tehran. The concessions Iran would have to make and the measures it would have to take in order to overcome Arab suspicions would be virtually inconceivable given Iran's domestic situation. The social composition of the area, the waning authority of some of the ruling families and Iran's manifest power all have the capacity to produce an atmosphere of suspicion. In December 1995, Iran's frustration with this state of affairs was given authoritative voice:

Saudi Arabia has always had a desire for domination in the region and the [West] has encouraged it to have this state of domination over the other five countries ... Who pursues this [island] issue? Saudi Arabia? Why? It wants to cover up its own hegemony. It has occupied Yemeni lands, it has occupied UAE lands, Qatari lands, Kuwaiti lands. It looks for another issue to cover up that one. Therefore, Saudi Arabia incites matters.[93]

III. IDEOLOGICAL COMPETITION: AN ISLAMIC COLD WAR

As Iran was reassessing its revolutionary excesses in the early 1990s, Islamic issues remained very much to the fore. Secular ideological schisms disappeared with the Cold War, leaving Islam with more scope and a greater potential role. Islamic solidarity was more prominent and potentially more politically significant than in the 1980s. Opportunities to represent, lead and shape the Islamic world in a new environment were also likely to increase competition between Iran and Saudi Arabia, representing the different concepts of what Islam stands for and the road it should follow.

Parallel to the end of the Cold War, by 1991 Iran had tired of crusades and faced the practical problems of reconstruction and economic planning. In diplomacy, this meant fence-mending and normalisation – but how much and at what cost? Iran, as the Islamic republic claiming to be a role-model, could scarcely be indifferent to Islamic issues. Recognition of Israel, for example, was unthinkable. 'The Islamic republic would have to change its name if it wanted to do such a thing. It cannot be a Muslim community and concede such an injustice'.[1]

As a Shi'i state, Iran has to try harder if it is to compete for a leadership role. This means taking positions, at least rhetorically, that are more 'extreme' or pure, less sullied by compromise or practical considerations. The Iranian leadership contrasts its own caring, 'striving', activist, self-reliant Islam with that of Saudi Arabia, depicted as conservative, selfish and dependent – one is independent, the other takes orders; one is liberated, the other servile.

This view finds its mirror-image in the comparison made by the Saudi authorities between their own interpretation of Islamic duties and those prevalent in the Islamic Republic of Iran. Asserting that 'the Koran and the Prophet's teachings are the constitution of the Kingdom of Saudi Arabia', King Fahd extolled the 'gentleness' of the social system founded upon those principles, the justice with which that system is imbued and the respect it enjoined for the wealth of the individual citizen. In international relations, the King continued, this meant that Saudi Arabia's 'relations with the rest of the world are at the best possible point because we do not interfere in anyone's affairs and do not want anyone to interfere in our affairs ... We want to be friends within the limits of our Islamic faith ... Nobody except God can impose his will on anyone'.[2]

By contrast, Iran's adherence to a more militant interpretation of Islamic obligation is portrayed as socially and politically disruptive and doctrinally perverse.

> Islam has never been, and never will be, a religion of conflict or clashes, violence or militancy. Defects in some communities are no justification for resorting to brutal force, destruction, transgressing all rights or following the law of the jungle. They can never justify any move to fan feelings of ill-will, tear common bonds to pieces, compromise national gains, blow up contradictions, annul the authority of the state, abuse its dignity or undermine the security of the country and its people.[3]

King Fahd, making these remarks in June 1993, seemed to have two targets in his sights – Iran, with which the perennial argument about permissible and impermissible behaviour during the *Hajj* was in full swing, and the Committee for the Defence of *Shari'a* Rights, established by a group of Saudi Islamist critics of the government in May 1993. This had enraged the ruling family, in part because Committee members had formed it publicly without first obtaining the King's permission but also in part because it called for the adoption of precisely the kind of radical, activist Islamic programme so dear to the hearts of the Iranian radicals.

Both Tehran and Riyadh try to justify their various positions – whether domestic or international – in terms of Islamic values and obligations. When these positions come into conflict each country must explain its differences in the language of Islam, suggesting that the other has a faulty understanding of 'true' Islam, either through ignorance, or, more frequently, through wilful misinterpretation. That Saudi Arabia is predominantly Sunni and Iran Shi'i enables both governments to inject – if only obliquely, since both are committed to the unity of the Islamic *umma*, or community – a note of sectarian prejudice into their arguments, knowing that this will find fertile ground in their respective populations. However, the particular sharpness which enters the dispute on Islamic issues has less to do with sectarian differences (for example, there are equally vituperative exchanges between Saudi Arabia and Sudan, both Sunni Muslim states) than with the *political* sensitivity of Islamic issues for both governments.

Decision-Making, Factionalism and Legitimacy
The tension between Iran's national interests and its ideology and values is always present. With no leader of stature comparable to Khomeini,

after 1991 the power structure was effectively divided between control of the government (President Rafsanjani) and the religious/revolutionary area (Rahbar Khamene'i).[4] Mirroring society's divisions, the leadership was split. Decision-making became an arena for consensus-building, debates and trade-offs, with consequent costs for the formulation of a consistent, coherent policy. All parties claimed that their positions adhered to Khomeini's attitude – 'the Imam's line'. Normally consensus was easiest to achieve on continuity rather than departure from past policy. Formulation of policy towards Saudi Arabia was not helped by such an arrangement; the issue of balancing national interests and values and the question of whether pursuing a revolutionary foreign policy further afield was compatible with normalisation, were posed especially starkly in the case of Saudi Arabia.

The Saudi authorities have, of course, long been aware of these competing demands. Apart from the material it has afforded their propaganda campaigns to underline the weakness and instability of the Iranian government, it has also caused them genuine anxiety, as the following 'responsible source' made plain in 1994.

> We are extremely astonished at the contradiction there is in the way the Iranian leaders are talking to us. While Ali Akbar Hashemi Rafsanjani, President of the Islamic Republic of Iran, continues to send his letters and his messengers to us with a view to improving relations and bringing closer viewpoints between the two countries, the spiritual leader, Ali Khamene'i, surprises us with improper and irresponsible statements, followed by a frenzied media campaign. Which of the two teams should we rely on and which of the two men should we deal with?[5]

Saudi Arabia must decide if the state-centred, practical and functional issues which could be the basis for bilateral cooperation might be jeopardised by the symbolic Islamic issues. At times the government of Saudi Arabia has also found it useful to speak with a number of voices. However, this is often a calculated move and only very rarely the outcome of genuine differences of opinion or contested authority within the ruling family.

For its part, Iran's decision-making system reflects the country's decentralised power structure; there is no dominant leader or centre and no clear focus for the revolution (after the war with Iraq). Foreign-policy issues have became entangled with personal rivalries, ideology and other considerations. For brevity its characteristics may be summarised as follows:

- The radical tendency in Iran sees everything as linked. Foreign policy is a yardstick for judging the regime's adherence to a revolutionary 'line', hence it is tied to domestic questions such as continued support for the *mustazefin* domestically, food subsidies, and such.
- However, reviving the economy is seen as a repudiation of the revolution's values; any normalisation with Saudi Arabia could lead to compromise with the United States.
- Decisions are reached by compromise and are periodically reviewed but never definitively settled. This means they are usually tactical rather than strategic and seen by neighbours as deceptive and unstable.
- Consensus on the prevailing line is easier than departure from it. Outside events can act as a catalysis to change (as in 1988 and 1990–91).
- The salience of ideological issues increases when Iran senses an opportunity or a threat. It also increases when blocked in other areas, such as economic development. Rafsanjani's continuing difficulties in the economic domain renders foreign policy an easier target for the radicals.
- There is a consensus that Iran is a key player on Islamic issues, but not on the price it should pay to remain in the leadership stakes.
- Pertinent to all Iran's foreign relations are the questions – do the moderates and radicals agree on the end but are separated only by a different view of the means?[6] Or are they genuinely different, with the moderates seeking to eschew export of the revolution and inch towards a normalisation with the world, as their opponents allege?

This continuing tug-of-war to define an Islamic foreign policy leads to an erratic course that satisfies no-one. The Iranian leadership is too divided or too uncertain of itself to impose one line. It may consider the costs of imposing discipline too high in terms of regime solidarity or it may not understand the necessity for clear choice. Perhaps it sees utility in keeping the militant option open and yet wants to lay claim to moderation. The net effect is to give the militants more influence on foreign policy. They can act as a *constraint* on official policy or as an *interest group* in a specific area, such as Iran's policy in Lebanon, Sudan and elsewhere.

They can act to *inhibit* policy initiatives (such as dialogue with the US); to *prevent* or delay actions, such as normalisation of relations with Saudi Arabia in 1991; or they may act as a *spoiler,* as in a few cases where government policy has been wrecked by an isolated act bearing the hallmarks of some governmental offshoot (e.g., Iranian pressures on Abu Musa in 1992). This domestic power struggle hurts Iran's relations with its Gulf neighbours, and there is no sign that any resolution is near.[7]

The troublesome implications of this for Iran–Saudi relations is that the militants see Saudi Arabia's 'subservient' Islam as anathema. A favourite issue is the mistreatment of the Kingdom's Shi'a.[8] In mid-1993, when Iran's improving relations with Saudi Arabia began to unravel, various pressure groups became active. Tehran University students, critical of the Foreign Ministry's (failing) policy of normalising relations with that country, insisted that Iran adhere to its Islamic principles and cited Saudi Arabia's advocacy of Wahabism as a reason to avoid 'close' relations.[9] It was perhaps significant that this coincided with the unusual step taken by the Saudi authorities of opening a dialogue with *Harakat Al-Islah* (the Reform Movement), a Saudi Shi'i group operating in exile. It appeared that the Saudi government hoped to reduce its exposure to such charges, and ensured that the Shi'i opposition did not make common cause with the recently formed Sunni opposition, embodied in the Committee for the Defence of *Shari'a* Rights. The negotiations proved successful, and in October 1993 an agreement was reached whereby the Reform Movement ceased publication of its highly critical, London-based magazine, *Jazirat Al-Arab* (*The Arabian Peninsula*). For its part, the Saudi government allowed the exiles to return, released a significant number of Shi'i detainees and lifted restrictions on the activities of others.[10] However, in Iran, the continuing vibrancy of the 'debate' is attested to by hardliners willing to question the revolutionary credentials of their opponents who were advocating *rapprochement* with Saudi Arabia. A leading radical came close to calling Rafsanjani's overtures to the Gulf states a betrayal of the revolution, saying his policies 'are not in line with the values and yardsticks of the Islamic revolution' or 'Khomeini's principles'.[11]

Iranian pragmatists, exemplified by Rafsanjani, have focused on national interest, the need for cooperation in OPEC and on security matters in the Persian Gulf. They emphasise the need for better bilateral relations to regularise the *Hajj* and to improve relations with the GCC, and seek to put the past behind them rather than cultivate grievances over it (such as the Mecca incident of 1987) which would only hinder future relations. Rafsanjani has referred to two trends within Iran on domestic and foreign policy which he termed leftist and rightist. He straddled the divide by emphasising the importance of eliminating foreign influences while arguing the need 'not to make enemies for ourselves ... we should not make enemies without any cause'.[12] This has been a recurrent theme. In 1991, when relations with Riyadh were restored, he cited changed conditions as the reason for departing from the explicit instructions in Khomeini's will. Rafsanjani argued that confrontational policies would only increase the Gulf states' dependency on the United States. 'Principally, it is in the interest of Islam and the region to be friends and cooperate with them'.[13]

The radicals implicitly believe that it is in Iran's interest to see a different – more popular and radical – regime in power in Saudi Arabia. They assume that such a regime would be more likely to make common cause with Iran, whose values it would share. The moderates' approach is formed by a different view. They do not see the current regime as necessarily temporary and want to repair working relations. Nor do they appear to share the view of their rivals that the substantive issues between Iran and Saudi Arabia would disappear with a change in regime in the Kingdom, hence they stress the need to address them bilaterally.

If there are geopolitical or structural limits to Iran–Saudi cooperation (but no equivalent limits to their scope for deterioration), then even a regime change can deliver only so much. It is true that the arrival of the IRI itself considerably worsened Iran–Saudi relations, not least by expanding their rivalry to Islamic leadership. Future Iran–Saudi relations would benefit from a positive change in Iran's attitude, but would they also benefit from a change in regime in Saudi Arabia towards a more radical model? Such a regime would also not accept Iran's Islamic leadership pretentions. Bilateral areas of contention, such as leadership in the Gulf and relations with the Gulf states would not vanish overnight. A different Saudi regime might treat the Saudi Shi'i community much worse than the current regime does.[14]

Despite the rhetoric of some radical elements in the Iranian political world, there is little reason for the Iranian government to do anything to encourage a change of regime in Saudi Arabia. If successful, the results might well be counterproductive; if unsuccessful, most of Iran's current strategies in the Gulf would be sabotaged. Of course, encouraging Saudi dissidents, whether Wahabi or Shi'i, may be the intention of government critics in Iran. This in turn questions Iran's ability to control its own radical offshoots; it is this weakness or uncertainity which worries the Saudi authorities as much as any perceived malign intent on the part of the current Iranian government.

The Hajj and Islamic Leadership

A important challenge to Saudi Arabia's claim to Islamic leadership is the *Hajj*. By 1991, both Iran and Saudi Arabia had interests in improving relations and resolving differences over Iran's participation in the annual pilgrimage. They agreed on the number of Iranian pilgrims allowed – 110,000 – as well as their right to hold a 'gathering' outside Mecca. Diplomatic ties were restored in March 1991 and both states hailed a 'new page' in relations.

The next two years' *Hajj* were relatively calm. Iranian pilgrims were restrained and held their gatherings at some distance from the main body of pilgrims as agreed, and Iranian leaders eschewed the inflammatory rhetoric of the past. Neither side could resist a certain amount of minor point scoring, but there were also conciliatory gestures by both.[15]

However, in May 1993 the *Hajj* agreement suddenly unravelled, with a renewed ban on demonstrations during the pilgrimage. In early May, the Committee for the Defence of *Shari'a* Rights made its appearance in Saudi Arabia. The emergence of this Saudi Islamist opposition group, headed by a number of establishment, Sunni (Wahabi) academics and lawyers from Nejd and Hijaz, alarmed the Saudi government which rapidly cracked down on the group – dismissing the government employees who joined the Committee and banning the lawyers from practising. In addition, in late May there were reports of about 400 people being arrested in connection with the Committee.[16]

The Saudi strictures on demonstrations during the *Hajj*, which infuriated the Iranians, were in part a reaction to these developments. Not only were they afraid there might be an adverse reaction to the arrests of the Islamists associated with the Committee during this emotional time, but they were also anxious to avoid the charge that, in turning a blind eye to Iranian demonstrations, they were being lenient to the Shi'a but tougher on the orthodox Wahabi Sunnis. Both for reasons of general public image in Saudi Arabia and politics within the ruling family, King Fahd wanted to avoid this charge, particularly as he was preparing to introduce political and administrative reforms.

There are also more general reasons for this deterioration in Saudi–Iranian relations. First, the agreement of 1991 was unclear; it had not clearly differentiated 'gatherings' from 'demonstrations' and it may be that Riyadh believed Iran was seeking to alter the definition. Second, good bilateral relations could not survive regional competition, especially the divergence on the Arab–Israeli peace process. Third, increasing animosity between the US and Iran was bound to translate into greater suspicion of Iran. Fourth, for purposes of GCC solidarity, Saudi Arabia could hardly embrace Tehran when it had a serious territorial issue with the United Arab Emirates.

A combination of these elements led to the breakdown of the *Hajj* agreement in May 1993. Nevertheless, the Saudi authorities continued to turn a blind eye to the demonstrations staged by Iranian pilgrims since the latter, rather than holding a public demonstration in Mecca, turned the memorial service for Khomeini, held at their camp in the desert at Mina, into the 'disavowal of infidels' ceremony that perennially upset the Saudi authorities. The Iranian media, in order to accentuate the drama, defiance and revolutionary virtue of the occasion, alleged that 'Saudi forces were hastily transferred to the area and encircled the venue of the rally. However, they had no chance for reaction as they had been caught by surprise'.[17] In fact, the Saudis did not intervene, pretending officially that it had not occurred, and the occasion passed peacefully.

Despite this restraint, the Iranian media and others used the occasion to denounce the Saudi regime as well as enemies closer to home. In responding to this, the Saudi authorities charged the Iranians with heresy for advocating a ceremony that 'totally contravenes the teachings of the Islamic religion and is fully outside the rules of the *Hajj* that had been laid down and explained by the messenger of God'. Some Iranians, they claimed, were

> ... insistent on disturbing the atmosphere and spreading confusion and disfiguring the great image of the faith by their practices that do not ... serve anything except their political plans and ideological aims'. This revealed the true intentions of the Iranian extremists and consequently undermined all positive efforts of wise Iranians who are keen on Iranian interests through their continuous attempts to soften the atmosphere between Iran and its Arab state neighbours, an effort that is welcomed by everyone.[18]

In the Saudi view, the 'wise Iranians who are keen on Iranian interests' began to lose ground markedly thereafter, and, unsurprisingly, the situation with regard to the *Hajj* deteriorated correspondingly. In

1994, Saudi Arabia again reintroduced the quota system, allowing only some 55,000 Iranian pilgrims into the Kingdom. As far as their conduct was concerned, Prince Nayef was adamant that, although the Iranians had declared that they would hold demonstrations, 'they will not be allowed to do so ... They have been informed of this decision and such acts will not be allowed to happen'.[19]

Under Saudi pressure and in order to avoid a bloody confrontation, Iran cancelled the scheduled demonstrations.[20] Iranians reacted in two distinct ways. Some, like leader Ali Khamene'i, emphasised that the key point in contention, namely the disavowal ceremony, was the symbol of activist Islam and resistance. 'The essential task of nations is to show their concern as regards the problems of the Islamic world in whatever way they can ... *What others do regarding oppressed nations is not our business ... I mean the inaction of others will not stop us*'.[21] A cleric expressed the dominant view. 'The Saudi army, Saudi oil, the Saudi state programme, even the religious speeches of Saudi speakers and management of holy sanctuaries are all under the supervision of America'.[22]

Iran, however, also showed a more conciliatory side. It reacted more with regret than anger and sought to reassure Saudi Arabia about Iranian motives for the demonstrations. Rafsanjani insisted that 'we shall not do anything contrary to the interests and security of [Saudi] Arabia ... If we raise this issue, we wish for the well-being of the [Saudi] Arabian nation and government'. Later, referring to their 'immaturity', he urged the Saudis to 'think harder about this issue'. While in favour of cooperation with all Islamic countries 'including [Saudi] Arabia ... we shall not retreat from our rights'.[23]

With the *Hajj* approaching in 1995, Iran again sought to increase the number of its pilgrims. Saudi Arabia now accepted 69,000, based on a quota system reflecting population size (versus the 110,000 it had accepted in the 1991 agreement). Iran sought to lift the ban on 'political gatherings' imposed by the Saudi authorities, arguing that the *Hajj* was a total event with political, social and religious experiences which could not be separated. As in the 1980s, Iran argued that Saudi reticence stemmed from its embarrassment that its allies, Zionism and the US, would be denounced.[24] Unlike the 1980s though, Iran gave way again to avoid clashes and cancelled its disavowal ceremonies.

The *Hajj* question, in which there is little intrinsically at stake, reflects the state of Iran's relations with Saudi Arabia.[25] When relations deteriorate, Iran can use this issue to apply pressure and reach a broader audience. Iran's attitude towards the *Hajj* also reflects its domestic situation and the competition to define its foreign policy. Those pushing a revolutionary line also seek a leadership role in Islam. In contrast, those seeking better relations with neighbours are more concerned about the costs of pursuing policies that might delay this. Since 1993, a tougher Saudi line rather than greater Iranian activism has once again brought the issue to the fore. This reflects concern about Iran's other activities in the region, but also indicates the general Saudi sensitivity on the resurgence of public Islamist dissent in Saudi Arabia itself.

This trend is reflected by two developments associated with the 1996 *Hajj*. The first was Saudi insistence on censoring and seizing any literature, books, printed material or pictures from the incoming pilgrims of all nationalities which the Saudi authorities disliked. By all accounts, the wide variety of texts seized, some of impeccably orthodox Muslim provenance, some of complete irrelevance to either the political or the moral sensibilities of the Kingdom, reflected an anxiety about the *Hajj* which went much further than fear of subversion. Second, it was noticeable that Iran officially took a conciliatory stance towards Saudi Arabia on the question of the *Hajj*.[26] In the 1996 *Hajj*, despite Iran's repeated assertions of its right to hold demonstrations, none were held. Saudi security forces were conspicuous and no clashes took place. The *Hajj* issue is indicative of much more than simply bilateral state-to-state relations. It also reflects the vicissitudes of domestic politics in both Iran and Saudi Arabia as these revolve around the issue of Islamic authority and authenticity. Consequently, it tells a good deal about the anxieties of both governments which fuel the sometimes acrimonious exchanges of the 'Islamic Cold War'.

The Arab–Israeli Issue and the Middle East Peace Process
No cause has greater symbolic appeal in the Islamic world than the plight of the Palestinians. Iranian leaders see it as an Islamic issue, giving them the right to be involved.[27] Framed as an Islamic, rather than an Arab issue, it offers Iran an entry point into the wider Middle East arena, since Iran can argue that this 'tragedy' stems from the failure to practise a true Islam. Iran offers a prescription for success – religious fervour, dedication and self-reliance – by pointing to its own experience and to the relative success of the Islamic resistance groups (such as *Hizbollah* or Islamic *Jihad* and *Hamas*) as opposed to the PLO.

The Iranian leadership believes in taking a strong stand on the issue, but leaves open the question of its own commitment. In October 1991 in

Tehran, at a conference of forces opposed to the Madrid peace process, Iranian radicals called for attacks on US facilities throughout the world. However, those in office counselled for more diplomacy and public denunciation of the process, while Khamene'i's position remained – as usual – midway between the two.[28] Since then Iran has cultivated ties with *Hamas* and Islamic *Jihad*, Sunni religious movements opposed to peace negotiations.

Iran sees the peace process as a significant betrayal of Islamic values. 'I believe', says Rafsanjani, 'that Palestine is the most important problem in the world and our history. It is only Iran, out of 180 countries in the world, which says that it does not accept the negotiations ...That is a basic source of pride for us'.[29]

While Iran argues that it will maintain an activist presence and treat the problems of other Muslims, including the Palestinians, as its own, it also uses these commitments as an excuse for its domestic problems. Iran's leaders attribute their deep unpopularity in the United States primarily to their principled stand on the Palestinian issue.[30]

Iran uses its opposition to the peace talks to warn the Arab states, notably Saudi Arabia. In assembling Arab governments around 'such a shameful negotiating table, it [the US] is facing its supporters ... with the wrath of their people'.[31] Iran was critical of Israeli participation in talks on the issue of water in Muscat under the auspices of the peace process in March 1994. Later, the Deputy Speaker of the Majlis condemned the lifting of the secondary commercial boycott of Israel as 'anti-Islamic'. The press reported that 'the Saudi regime is trying to improve the Zionist regime's image among Middle East Arab states under instructions from the US'.[32] Iranian leaders warned Arab leaders against making peace with Israel, claiming that their people would 'never accept their leaders' treason or remain silent'.[33] To support this, the Iranian media reported student demonstrations in Saudi Arabia criticising the government's 'informal compromise' with the 'Zionist regime'. It also criticised Saudi Arabia's senior *mufti* for issuing a *fatwa* stating that a permanent peace with the 'Zionist entity, which is usurping the land of Palestine, is permissible'.[34]

Saudi Arabia has supported the peace process since the Madrid summit in 1991, but it has continually been preoccupied with the question of balance between regional allies who may have rejected the peace process with Israel, and its major ally the US, which promoted it. The danger for the Saudi government was that its own alliance with the US would become an embarrassment in the event of Arab–Israeli armed conflict. The choices forced upon Saudi Arabia divided the ruling family. King Fahd, when he was still Crown Prince, was associated with the trend in Saudi royal family politics which advocated recognition of Israel (in the Fahd Plan of 1981) in order to reach a comprehensive settlement.

The defeat of Iraq, the prostration of the PLO and the emergence of Syria as an ally of the Western powers in the 1991 Gulf War created conditions for an Arab consensus on the need to negotiate peace with Israel. The process itself, in the form of the Washington talks, stalled, threatening a return to the *status quo ante* which had been so uncomfortable for the Saudi government. It was, consequently, not surprising that Saudi Arabia supported the Oslo accords and the Declaration of Principles that followed in 1993. This was justified on the basis of their belief that the Gaza–Jericho agreement represented 'a Palestinian–Israeli step toward peace which we consider a prelude to endorsing the Palestinian people's legitimate rights', because 'struggle from inside provides a better opportunity for independence than resistance from the diaspora states'.[35] As far as other issues were concerned, the Saudi government generally echoed Syrian demands for a complete Israeli withdrawal from the Golan Heights and a full and unconditional withdrawal of Israeli forces from Lebanon.

Momentum seemed to be building for a comprehensive peace settlement in the Middle East, thus laying the foundation for reconciliation between Saudi Arabia and Chairman Yasser Arafat, who had blotted his copybook by supporting Iraq during the Gulf crisis and war. In contrast to Iran, Saudi Arabia tended to treat the whole Palestine–Israeli issue as the struggle of the Palestinian people for their national rights and the struggle of the Arab world at large for the restoration of territories occupied in 1967. This was not simply a tactical manoeuvre, but indicated the importantance of its regional constituency – the Arab world. Domestically, Saudi Arabia also sought to emphasise the Arab nature of the issue; the danger of presenting it solely as an Islamic issue would, in theory, make it possible for Saudi Islamist radicals to 'outbid' their government. As *Hamas* and the other Palestinian radical Islamist opposition movements have discovered, it is best to be an opposition movement, powerless but also free of the responsibilities of power.

However, the Saudi government could not shy away entirely from the Islamic overtones of the conflict and sought to affirm its own commitment to the Islamic issues at stake. It frequently reiterated its support for the return of the Holy Places of Jerusalem to Islamic, Palestinian control; its reconciliation with Arafat took place in the context of his performance of the *'umra*, or minor pilgrimage to Mecca. It also sought and received a *fatwa* from the senior *mufti*, Sheikh Bin Baz, stating that peace between Muslims and Jews was compatible with the *shari'a* and the example of the Prophet. This move was clearly intended to legitimate the growing involvement of Saudi Arabia and its GCC allies with Israel in the peace process by lifting the secondary and tertiary boycotts against Israel in 1994 and by hosting some sessions of the multilateral talks in Oman and Qatar.

This strategy was chiefly aimed at domestic critics of the Saudi government's involvement in the peace process.[36] There may have been some consideration of the impact this would have in the wider Islamic world, as well, but Bin Baz' judgment was only likely to carry significant weight within Saudi Arabia itself. The more characteristic Saudi response to Iranian commentary on, or interference in the Arab–Israeli conflict is encapsulated in the following comment in *Al-Nadwah*:

> The Iranian regime ... went on to bark through its mass media, attacking this virtuous country and the sons of the Gulf region, to the extent that its barking extended to the whole Arab world because everyone has isolated it from the movements and meetings which have taken place in the Arab region. Iran considered that one of its legitimate rights, as though it was an Arab country with a direct or indirect link to this thorny issue which belongs to the Arabs alone.[37]

Most Iranians probably believe that Iran should be a leader on Islamic issues, and hence in competition with Saudi Arabia, yet there is no national, grass-roots consensus on Palestine which forces the regime's hand. Most likely, the leadership manipulates the issue for its own purposes. Similar considerations prevail on other Islamic issues. Iran likes to take extreme stands, as in its 1993 offer of 10,000 troops to help the Bosnian Muslims. Whether in Central Asia, the Occupied Territories or Afghanistan, Iranian activism and the impulse to 'have a presence' has pitted Iranian resources and influence against those of Saudi Arabia. However, although there is a sense of innate rivalry in some areas, the degree to which it is pursued often depends on the state of relations in other areas. Thus on Afghanistan, the signing of the Pakistan-brokered accord between the various Afghan factions in Mecca in March 1993 preceded a visit to Iran by the Pakistani premier and the Afghan leaders. The occasion was used to extol pan-Islamic (including Iranian) cooperation.[38.]At the time, relations between Iran and Saudi Arabia were relatively harmonious. However, the tone changed markedly by 1994, when Iran–Saudi suspicion and mistrust resurfaced. The Afghan accord had by then itself unravelled, and Iran was now accused of having 'kindled the fire in Afghanistan and ... [having come] between the *jihad* brothers, divided them and torn them apart'.[39]

Iran no longer concentrates on Shi'i groups and hopes now to build on ties with opposition Sunni forces. It has difficulty rejecting groups that solicit resources from it or denying some link with groups opposed to governments, as in Egypt or Algeria. It sees the upsurge in Islamic movements in the Middle East as inspired by its own model and as a 'tribute to its revolution'.[40] It claims more than it can deliver, if only because its resources are limited and the Shi'i/Sunni divide remains. Nevertheless, Iran believes that Islam is a more important factor for cohesion than nationalism or ethnicity.

Islam and National Interest

In terms of the reassertion of Islamic values in late twentieth-century politics, Iran remains a potent force. It retains its attraction as a revolutionary model and as a source of funds for opposition groups. Unable to attract others by example or ideology, Iran can nonetheless tap into the discontent of other societies, eroding the legitimacy of their governments by alluding to their dependency, materialism and cultural contamination. Because of its capacity to point out ambiguities between the Saudi ruling dynasty's position as worldly monarchs and as guardians of the two Holy Places (and by association, of Islam more generally), it is able to touch an already sensitive nerve in the Kingdom. Consequently, the Iranian threat is one which can increase or decrease according to the situation in the Kingdom itself, and may turn on how the Saudis handle their domestic political transitions.

In 1996 there were a number of reasons for the Saudi ruling family to feel sensitive on this score. Although the eventual succession of Crown Prince Abdullah was never in dispute, in order to avoid the paralysis of government caused by his own illness, King Fahd prematurely delegated his executive powers to Abdullah in January 1996. This brought out the latent rivalry between the most powerful members of the Al Saud (the 'Sudayri', or full brothers of the King), protective of their fiefdoms and concerned that Abdullah would erode their power. Within a couple of months, the King, although still far from well, took back his powers, reportedly at the behest of his brothers.

The possible dangers of uncertainty or indecision were underlined in April by the trial of four men accused of bombing the National Guard building in Riyadh in November 1995. According to Saudi intelligence, a network of dissidents existed, fired by Islamist ideals and willing to use violence, linked to such figures as Usama Bin Laden and Abu Muhammad Issam Al-Makdissi through their connections with the Mujahedin in Afghanistan. The men were executed in May 1996, but as if to drive home the scale of the problem, a massive bomb exploded at US housing in the Saudi military compound at Al-Khobar on 25 June, killing 19 US military personnel. This was accompanied by claims from obscure groups that the bomb was in revenge for the May executions and by promises that further violence would follow until the US withdrew its forces from the Kingdom.

The significance of these developments in the context of the Iran–Saudi relationship is twofold. First, they emphasise the lengths to which dissidents in Saudi Arabia will go in order to protest the Saudi–US relationship. Iran may be encouraged by this. Although there is no sign that the Saudi government intends to change its policies, there may be those in Iran who believe that if sufficient momentum can be created, the Saudi–US link can indeed be weakened, if not broken. Second, the US reaction to these events may well have an impact on Iran–Saudi relations, either from reported nervousness by the US government as it contemplated its strategic investment in the area, or because of the conclusions it may draw from the apparent similarity between the bombers' goals and those of the Iranian government which also wants to see US forces leave the Gulf. These developments are unlikely to weaken the regime in Saudi Arabia, but they clearly undermine confidence and help create an atmosphere of mistrust across the Gulf.

In fact, however, Iran's threat is ebbing; 17 years after seizing power, its Islamic appeal has surely peaked. It is no longer seen as a model for government, since it has failed to deliver. Its pragmatism has circumscribed its appeal. In addition, it has largely failed to transcend its narrow Shi'i support base, and even this sectarian constituency is not always united. As differences on the choice of successor for the *Marja'iyya* (senior Shi'i cleric) in 1993 demonstrate, the Shi'a are not only divided but split nationally and between Arabs and Persians. (Iran prefers to keep the leadership Iranian and at Qom; many Arab Shi'a see Najaf and its grand ayatollahs in Iraq as more worthy of leadership.)[41]

Iran is thus unable even to 'deliver' its Shi'i clientele, especially where there is competition. Iran could not compete with the Saudi state for influence with the Saudi Shi'a once the Saudi government decided to cultivate rather than antagonise the Shi'a-based 'Reform Movement' in 1993. In view of the Saudi government's concessions to and investment in the Shi'a of the Eastern Province, the cultivation of links with Iran served little purpose.

However, official Saudi cultivation of its Shi'i community was in part a response to more general problems that emerged in the 1990s. Since its foundation, the rulers of Saudi Arabia have faced sporadic challenges from those who believe that the policies of the state do not conform with the Islamic ideal. In the late twentieth century this has taken the form of indictment of the autocratic and irresponsible nature of the Saudi monarchy, denunciation of the inegalitarian distribution of wealth and of the corruption of some members of the House of Saud, as well as criticisms of the close alignment between Saudi Arabia and the United States. It has been suggested that preoccupation with dynastic ambitions and personal enrichment has caused the Al Saud to stray further than is permissible from the true path of Islamic rectitude.

Using distinctively Islamic political language, these critical voices do not differ much from other populist, Islamist critiques throughout the Middle East, and they appear to Saudi authorities to be part of the same general movement of Islamist radicalism. Thus, whether the criticism comes from the Iranian media or a group within Saudi Arabia, the Saudi authorities may see an organisational link, when in fact the connection may simply be that the criticisms of the ruling family are similar. Ironically, at a time when Iran's threat as an Islamic revisionist power may be receding, the vulnerability – and thus sensitivity – of the Saudi regime on questions of Islamic propriety and authority may be increasing.

The Iranian government also uses Islam as a legitimating device, important for a state that has little to show its people. Its exertions on the Palestine issue represent an effort to expand Iran's otherwise limited political base by appealing to Muslims at large. Pragmatism, however, tempers Iran's approach; there is no sign that Iran is willing to sever ties with Syria, a 'strategic ally', merely because that state may reach a peace agreement with Israel. Similarly, Iran's fire-and-brimstone rhetoric is not matched by a willingness to get involved militarily against Israel. Indeed, it has specifically disavowed any such intention.[42]

Despite its use of Islamic vocabulary and imagery, revolutionary Iran has shown no tendency to forswear national interest for Muslim solidarity. Its attitude towards the dispute over Abu Musa is a traditional one, not noticeably different from that of the Shah. Iran views Saudi Arabia through the lens of its own conflict with the United States; equally, Saudi concerns about Iran tend to revolve around its military capabilities and intentions. In this context, the US forces in the Gulf play 'a counterweight to the Iranian challenge'.[43] From this perspective, the ideological differences are secondary; when constrained, Iran will readily drop the Islamic emphasis. It has established good relations in the Central Asian and transcaucasian states by building on cultural connections rather than Muslim ties. Tehran has shown a marked reluctance to endanger state-to-state relations with Russia, even to the point of playing down its reaction to Russian intervention against Muslims in Tajikistan and Chechnya.

Does this selective use of Islam suggest that Iran uses ideology opportunistically? Not necessarily. Iran's clerical leaders doubtless believe their own utterances. Depending on the issue at hand, Islam is accordingly exploited or played down; the same might be said of Saudi Arabia's leaders. Islamic values form part of the political culture of Saudi Arabia, both amongst the elite and in the population at large. Government initiatives must therefore be presented in light of the contribution they make to realising certain Islamic ideals. However, this does not mean that service to Islam is the sole motive for political action, either within the Kingdom or in its foreign policy. On the Saudi, as on the Iranian, side there are other priorities at work, unwilling as both regimes may sometimes be to admit this basic fact of political life.

In theory, and sometimes officially, Islam can be portrayed in both countries as a potential bridge across the shores of the Persian Gulf, spanning the chasm between Arab and Persian and mending the rift between Sunni and Shi'a. In practice, the situation is rather different. Disputes between the states may not have stemmed from ideological differences, but they have been exacerbated by them; expressed in the language of Islam, they form the basis of national rivalry. The causes of Iran–Saudi tensions are neither ideological nor are they to be found in their different views of Islam. However, the intrusion of these tensions into this rivalry has caused a more bitter and divisive relationship. Each regime has the capacity to touch a raw nerve in the other over the degree to which its behaviour adheres to an Islamic ideal. They can touch these nerves effectively because of the ambivalences in their own position –

ambivalences which their domestic and external critics spend much time highlighting. Improving relations will thus be less dependent on a change of policy than on a change in regime, and even then, much will depend on the nature of the successor.

IV. OIL POLITICS, REVENUES AND ECONOMIC SECURITY

Economic issues, including oil, are of great political importance both to Iran and Saudi Arabia, although in different ways. In Iran, initially, Islamic leaders attempted to deny that the revolution would be judged by its economic performance. However, years of war and destruction, rapid population growth, corruption and indifferent economic management have sapped Iranians' support for further sacrifice. The population is simply unwilling to accept more hardship. With the pressing needs of reconstruction, the demands of a burgeoning population and the decline in fervour among the revolution's faithful, the political salience of economic development has grown. Underscoring this is the number of scattered protests and riots over economic conditions in the country since 1992.

Saudi leaders have never been under any illusion about the importance of economic resources. They have learned in the past decade or so that the role of the state as universal provider of goods and services may have to be reduced. Even with massive funds at its disposal, the state has found that it cannot at a time of depressed oil revenues meet all of its commitments as easily as once it could. Instead, it must make choices and prioritise. This has had an impact on the expectations of a population used to a lavish scale of public subsidies and well aware of the ruling family's conspicuous wealth. This process has been particularly marked since the 1991 Gulf War, with the enormous costs of that effort and a continuing 'softness' of oil prices.[1]

The Saudi strategy has been to maximise oil revenues by maintaining production at a high level. Saudi Arabia is determined that its own oil production should not fall below 8 mb/d and that it should retain its 35% share of OPEC production. At the same time it is unwilling to press for dramatic rises in the price of oil. This is partly because of Saudi concern about the effect of this on the West's industrialised economies, the consequences for future oil demand (and Saudi revenues), and the US–Saudi relationship. However, its unwillingness is also due to the Saudi government's awareness that a significant rise in oil prices could only be achieved by a dramatic reduction in its own oil production, given the poor discipline of OPEC and the growing volume of non-OPEC production.

The Iranian regime, determined to reduce its reliance on oil income, has been unable to provide a political environment conducive to developing the private sector, and has thus been unable to realise this reduction. Oil revenues have fluctuated dramatically over the past decade, with a steady trend downwards. In real terms, oil was cheaper in 1995 than in 1973. In constant terms, the price of oil in 1994 was $20 per barrel; in 1995 it had fallen to $15–17 per barrel (versus $40 in 1983–84).[2] For Iran, this situation posed serious problems. Inflation in 1995 ran at nearly 60%.[3] Per capita GDP has fallen 50% and per capita earnings from oil, in real terms, are no more than one-quarter of the pre-revolutionary level.[4] The hardest period for Iran's economy, which is trying to service a short term debt of roughly $5–7bn a year until 2000, coincides with the anticipated period of low oil prices.[5]

Problems compound one another; Iran has barely maintained its oil fields well enough to sustain a high level of production. To maximise its production capacity – or even to maintain it – Iran needs cash, yet the current situation does not allow for such vital investments. These either have to be postponed or paid for by committing Iran's future oil production. Equally grave are the political constraints that prevent Iran from cutting its profligate domestic oil subsidies that lead to waste, smuggling and substantial loss in income.[6] At current rates of domestic consumption Iran may not have much oil available for export by the year 2000.[7] Low oil prices have forced cutbacks, but the prospect of Iraq's return to the market hangs over and depresses the market, which would be further affected if it occurs before demand rises.[8] This was confirmed by the lowering effect on prices after Iraq's acceptance of UN Security Council Resolution 986 in mid-1996, allowing it to export $2bn of oil. Furthermore, the economic embargo imposed on Iran by the United States in 1995 has forced Iran to find alternative markets for its crude oil. Despite initial bravado, there are signs (such as the renting of South African storage facilities) that Iran has experienced difficulties adjusting to the embargo.

Iran is thus facing a five-year period of austerity which could become a major economic crisis with political repercussions. How Iran responds to this, whether by increased cooperation in OPEC or by a more belligerent attitude towards its neighbours, remains to be seen. For price and revenue stability, cooperative relations with Saudi Arabia would appear to be imperative. This will have to include agreement on how to accommodate Iraq's full re-entry to the oil market, and will involve an agreement on how to allocate cuts in production[9]. Yet this will not be easy to achieve.

In 1990–91 Saudi Arabia, with the largest (spare) production capacity, quickly stepped into the gap created by the absence of Kuwait and Iraq from the market, and softened the shock effect on prices. Since the mid-1980s, the Kingdom has otherwise refused to act as the swing producer, reducing or increasing its production to suit OPEC or the market. It now insists that production levels be decided not according to historic levels, or income need, but by production capacity. The Saudi argument was fortified by its uniquely strong position during 1991–92. It devoted considerable resources to improving its refining capacity to ensure that it could produce 10 mb/d by 1995. In fact, this target was achieved by 1993, giving it a total capacity of 10–11 mb/d, versus the 8 mb/d it produced, allowing it a spare capacity unmatched by any other state. With bargaining power in the cartel flowing from oil production capacity, the Saudis, producing one-third of OPEC's output, needs OPEC less than the other members.[10]

Iran, with large revenue needs, little sympathy for the West, insufficient reserves to take a long-term view of the market and production at maximum capacity, saw Saudi oil policy as an extension of its alliance with the US. There are some grounds for this interpretation. There is at least an implicit understanding that Saudi Arabia will keep oil prices low in exchange for US protection.[11] To Iran, this represents (ideology apart) a real problem. Iran cannot match Saudi influence within OPEC and needs Saudi cooperation. Whether it can generate any compensating leverage that does not alienate Saudi Arabia is doubtful.

Since 1991, Saudi Arabia has assumed a dominant role in oil politics.[12] Iran's attempts to match this by increasing its productive capacity in order to recapture its pre-revolutionary role as an OPEC leader, have been to no avail. Simply put, without Saudi cooperation Iran has been unable to achieve its own economic and political goals, which are not necessarily compatible with those of Saudi Arabia.

In 1993, when prices slid to a five year low and Iran's much-needed oil revenues melted away, Tehran sought to pressure Saudi Arabia to cut production in order to accommodate Kuwait. Iran accused Saudi Arabia of over-production; Saudi Arabia in turn accused Iran (and Nigeria) of 'chronic large-scale cheating on quotas'.[13] OPEC's divisions accelerated the price slide. By autumn 1993, Iran took a different tack.

Reflecting the sensitivity of the free fall in prices and revenues, Iran sought to avoid further quarrels which would continue to weaken the market. President Rafsanjani contacted King Fahd directly before the September 1993 OPEC meeting to arrange a compromise. The outcome was an agreement which presented a solid OPEC front, strengthening prices while boosting Iran's quota from 3.3 mb/d to 3.6 mb/d.[14] It was reportedly achieved because Saudi Arabia agreed to give up some of its market share to Iran, although it refused any suggestion that its production should fall below 8 mb/d. It further agreed that Iran's quota should thenceforth be close to what it was already producing, thereby legitimating Iran's *de facto* rule breaking.[15] The Iranian decision to seek accommodation with the Saudis bore the hallmarks of Rafsanjani's pragmatism. Isolating Iran's need to cooperate with Saudi Arabia on oil from differences on other matters was not easy. Nevertheless, the September 1993 OPEC meeting demonstrated that cooperation, when tried, could be beneficial to all.

Saudi Arabia's willingness to cut its own production enough both to placate Iran and to increase prices did not appear to harm it economically, since the small rise in prices tended to cover the small cut in Saudi production. For Iran, however, there was an advantage on both counts and this consideration appears to have weighed most heavily with the Saudi authorities. It was a period when acrimony over the 1993 *Hajj* had passed and thoughts were turning to the 1994 *Hajj*. It also coincided with Saudi negotiations with political dissidents from its Shi'i minority in an attempt to bring them back into the fold – an objective achieved soon after the September OPEC meeting. In addition, both sides had now delineated their respective positions on Abu Musa and the Tunbs. It is possible that the concession to Iran at OPEC was intended to create an atmosphere in which compromise over the islands could be achieved, dangling in front of the Iranians enticing possibilities of what might be gained in the realm of oil production and prices if cooperation and goodwill existed between Iran and Saudi Arabia.

Goodwill was evident in January 1994 when the *Tehran Times* called for further cooperation by the two states in OPEC and on regional matters. 'What counts are the decisions reached by the leaders of the two countries regarding the creation of cordial relationships'. King Fahd sent a personal emissary to Rafsanjani that same month.[16] He was warmly received and Rafsanjani took the opportunity to stress that 'regional issues, as well as falling world oil prices ... [are] among the most basic issues that warrant cooperation among all Muslim countries, especially Iran and Saudi Arabia'. The Iranian media spoke of 'a new phase of bilateral ties designed to reinforce unity among Islamic countries and overcome the problems of the Islamic world', stressing the need for cooperation in oil production with a view to 'checking the falling price of oil'.[17]

The honeymoon was not to last. Within a month, the same media were criticising Saudi Arabia for extravagant purchases in the US, suggesting that Saudi Arabia had embarked on over-production in order to appease the US.[18] The Saudis, in turn, refuted Iranian allegations, stating that 'the Kingdom adheres to its allotted quota and to all the agreements it signs. In contrast, Iran ... adheres to its quota only when it is incapable of production ... the untrustworthy Iranian oil policy has become a source of annoyance inside OPEC and helped prices to fall over the past four months'.[19] With neither trusting the other to abide by a quota, each accused the other of over-production.[20]

This rapid deterioration in relations was an inauspicious prelude to the March 1994 OPEC meeting when Iran sought, but failed to achieve further cuts in Saudi production. This led to denunciations of Saudi Arabia, specifically accusing the government of giving higher priority to the interests of the US than to those of its own people or of its neighbours. Iranian officials believed that Saudi actions were part of a 'dastardly ... scheme' intended to weaken Iran and its support for just causes.[21] The Saudis insisted that their policies, if they were to be stable, could not depend on short-term calculations, or, in an allusion to Iran's economic crisis, on 'special considerations and circumstances through which some countries are passing and which prompt them to [pursue] practices harmful to all'.[22]

The record of the past few years has tended to demonstrate that Saudi Arabia is capable of and willing to cooperate with Iran on questions of oil pricing and production only if it believes that this cooperation is producing beneficial effects in other areas as well. This is because such cooperation is usually a Saudi commitment either to cut production or not to raise it at certain times, thereby risking a fall in revenue. However, the scale of these cuts has not been seen as adequate to fulfil Iran's desperate need for revenue. Iran will remain sensitive to economic conditions, vulnerable to weakness in the oil market and factors reducing their oil revenues unless it can devise a promising, alternative strategy for influencing the oil market. Those Iranian officials who can negotiate a cooperative agreement with Saudi Arabia on oil production/ pricing may be in no position to offer Saudi Arabia the pragmatic *quid pro quo* that it seeks in other areas. If pragmatism prevails, Tehran will try to keep a cooperative relationship with Saudi Arabia in this area insulated from other areas of rivalry. Whether Saudi Arabia will accept this compartmentalisation is an altogether different question.

CONCLUSION

Prospects for Iran–Saudi Relations

Iran's revolution and its accompanying foreign policy have made an always difficult relationship with Saudi Arabia worse. To competition for influence in the Persian Gulf has been added rivalry over competing conceptions of Islam and influence in other areas, such as the Palestinian territories. Hostility towards the United States and its presence in the region exacerbates the situation. The experience of the past 17 years has increased Iran's sense of grievance, making it oblivious to the degree to which its actions have increased its neighbours' sense of insecurity. Yet, in the case of Saudi Arabia at least, that very sense of insecurity has led its government to an increasingly close military relationship with the US, which Iran perceives as a direct threat to its own interests.

A different, nationalist Iran might pose problems for Saudi Arabia, but of a conventional sort – competition for power and influence which could be met by balancing alliances, cooperation and diplomacy. Such an Iran would enter into temporary alliance with its neighbour and could be an acceptable ally, for example, against the greater threat posed to both states by Iraq. Islamic Iran is a different matter. It cannot be as flexible or as dependable; above all, it cannot be trusted by Saudi Arabia. Not only are its aims potentially less limited than its nationalist counterpart, but, from the Saudi reading of impulses at work in Iran, these goals include the fundamental re-ordering of the Saudi political system. This makes establishing an indigenous balance of power of the two states against a putative aggressor impossible today, whereas it was a reality in the 1970s when a nationalist Iran existed. However ambitious it might have been, Iran under the Shah had no political aspirations in Saudi Arabia.

Economically and militarily weaker than in the past, Iran is not equipped to compete commercially in the post-Cold War world. Its claim to represent a correct, authentic, caring, activist and independent Islam puts it in direct competition with Saudi Arabia. Iran is under pressure to perpetuate this role for two reasons. First, as the only Shi'i state it has to work hard to authenticate its Islamic credentials and to have any influence beyond its small sectarian constituency. Second, strong positions on Islamic issues are important for the regime's legitimacy. 'Having a presence', 'striving', showing solidarity with the oppressed, 'confronting the arrogant' are basic elements in the regime's lexicon and cannot be discarded casually, especially as it has precious little else to offer its supporters.

It is also important for the Saudi ruling family to demonstrate its concern both for Islamic values and for Islamic issues world wide. They have had to adopt multiple strategies to deal with these topics – strategies which have been geared not only to meet the challenge of Iran, but also to placate constituencies in Saudi Arabia. These might have little sympathy with Iran, but might agree with the tone and substance of some of the radical Iranian criticisms of the Saudi government.

The legacy of the past decade and a half has made reconciliation harder, but there are no signs that Iran wants an appreciably different approach to regional relations. The struggle for power in Iran, together with the regime's essentially decentralised nature, make for erratic policies. Contradictory statements and actions make it harder for neighbours to assess Iran's intentions, consequently they judge its deeds. Growing economic problems do little to increase confidence that the Iranian leadership will change course, except perhaps to accommodate radicals by diversionary forays. There is, in short, no sign that its distinctive Islamist ideology or its volatility will diminish.

For Saudi Arabia this is a worrying prospect. It realises that it is at the forefront of much of the ideologically motivated criticism that surfaces in Iranian public life, including questions about the monarchy and privilege, the claim to Islamic virtue or the evils of foreign – that is, US – intervention in the region. Furthermore, political volatility in Iran will keep the Saudi government guessing about Iran's true intentions at any particular moment and will shadow any agreement reached, suggesting that the slightest appearance of amity or cooperation will simply be transient. There still exists a conviction either that Iran's long-term intentions remain fundamentally inimical to the political order in Saudi Arabia, or that, in the maelstrom of Iranian politics, those espousing radically critical views of the Kingdom will direct state policy. The uncertainty is born out of the difficulty – shared by the Saudis with many – of foreseeing which will be the dominant interpretation of Iran's role in the region at any given time.

In light of the ambiguous messages Iran has sent out over the years, there is little doubt that a US security guarantee has become more than simply desirable – in the eyes of many Saudi policy-makers it has become a necessity. For this visible and reassuring short-term security presence the Saudi government is willing to incur continuing Iranian wrath (as well as violent opposition within the Kingdom). Although the presence of the US might aggravate Iranian authorities, the Saudi regime strongly suspects that its very presence as a ruling dynasty, with different interpretations of Islamic obligation, is aggravation enough.

Future regional crises could see Iran the beneficiary. Iran's reaction will be opportunistic because it will be hard to resist exploitable situations, especially if they promise to revive a flagging revolution or add to Iran's power in some sense. To reassure its neighbours, Iran needs to rule out such behaviour in advance – something it is not willing to do. Thus, disturbances since 1994 in Bahrain have been attributed to 'foreign hands', whether or not Iran is actually involved. Yet, Iran's reputation (and record) is such that suspicions are raised about *any* disturbance whether in Bahrain, Saudi Arabia or elsewhere – a useful alibi for local states perhaps, but a serious impediment to improved relations between Iran and the GCC.

How are Iran's national interests in the Gulf in conflict with its ideological imperative and what price is Iran willing to pay to pursue the latter? Iran wants good relations with Saudi Arabia and the GCC, but only on its own terms. It is unwilling to renounce its commitment to a 'fair' Palestinian settlement, effectively denying the legitimacy of the state of Israel. It will insist on taking a stand on issues affecting Muslims, from Algeria to Bosnia, and will continue to agitate against the United States (and Zionism) as symbols of oppression and arrogance.

Clearly, Iran's terms will not allow easy, let alone good, relations with Saudi Arabia, particularly since they cannot 'agree to disagree'. Iran will persist with policies that are ambiguous if not directly hostile. It will emphasise bilateralism and play on the differences among the GCC states. Its policies will resemble those of a 'spoiler', opposed to others' initiatives but without any positive aim. Iran offers no alternative design for organising the region to further joint interests.

In the Saudi experience, conciliatory initiatives towards Iran have tended to end in one of two ways. They have come up against a series of unacceptable demands about larger issues – such as breaking the Saudi alliance with the US – which the Iranian government says are necessary preconditions for any initiative. Alternatively, they have fallen victim to the ideological debate within Iranian politics which can seize small issues and turn them into questions of great symbolic power.

In the absence of a stable, confidence-building relationship with Saudi Arabia, Iran has fallen back on promoting Arab fragmentation and reacting to regional opportunities. In reality, Iranian 'policy' is principally a series of stands and declarations reflecting positions congenial to the leadership. It does not reflect a considered position related to identified interests, priorities or a cost-benefit analysis. Consequently, Iran–Saudi relations will continue to be turbulent.

That said, under what conditions might there be scope for change in Iran–Saudi relations? On Iran's side a significant change in the dynamics of domestic politics or a marked departure in relations with the United States could precipitate such a change. De-Islamisation or the secularisation of foreign policy, with greater emphasis on national interest, diminished activism and less posturing in foreign relations, would be elements in this change. Greater pragmatism and more emphasis on building confidence with its neighbours would be another manifestation. The most likely cause of this change would come from domestic transformations, such as an increased centralisation of power or a new national consensus resulting from widespread recognition of and reaction to the economic penalties of continuing current policies, perhaps generated by a sudden economic shock and its political consequences.

With the largely reactive and frequently defensive attitude that currently characterises Saudi policy towards Iran, Saudi Arabia would respond cautiously to such a change. It is unlikely to take any initiative itself to change the current nature of Iran–Saudi relations, principally because of its inability to effect the kinds of changes that would make a difference. As far as its security relationship with the United States is concerned, a marked improvement in Iran–US relations would change the context of Saudi–US relations. However, it is unlikely to change the perceived need in Saudi Arabia to continue close relations, since that need does not derive simply from the perceived Iranian threat.

Since the Iranian revolution, Riyadh has been alone in seeking privileged relations with Washington. Before 1979, Tehran was the United States' favourite ally; it may be again one day. Although that day is not yet in sight, the idea of good Iran–US relations must be considered in Riyadh with mixed feelings. On the one hand, it would mean a diminution in the threat from Iran; on the other the beginning of diplomatic rivalry for Washington's ear and the loss of Saudi influence. That preconditions for such a shift do not currently exist does not alter the belief among most of the Saudi ruling elite that it is in their interests to keep Iran and the United States apart. Others disagree and would prefer to establish a different kind of game in which both Saudi Arabia and Iran could be allies of the United States. This is of little immediate significance for regional policies, but it may herald a future change of direction as a younger generation of the Al Saud come to power.

The Conditions for Regional Order

The Persian Gulf has seen violent change in recent years. A revolution and two wars have generated the dynamics which buffet the region. The end of the Cold War left the United States, the unchallenged superpower, to act as the region's balancing power, the region having demonstrated in recent years its inability to maintain its own balance. The challenge today is to fashion a provisional system with external assistance, while encouraging the development of a regional substitute.

Historically, an outside power – the UK – maintained regional order. British paramountcy was replaced by a three-cornered competition among the Gulf's major powers – Iran, Iraq and Saudi Arabia. Each of these states has at different times been a hegemonic power: Wahabi Saudi Arabia, Ba'athist Iraq and Khomeinist Iran. Relations between these states after the mid-1970s were upset by Iran's revolution and the resultant instability. Initially, Iran's threat to the region was contained by Iraq, together with the GCC and an external coalition of Arabs and Western states. Then Iraq's threat was contained by a coalition comprising regional and distant states, led by the United States. The United States thus became the heir to the UK's role – the manager of order in the Gulf.

US policy is to build up the GCC states through arms transfers and training, to 'take down' Iraq and Iran's military capabilities through trade sanctions and to maintain a significant military presence to reassure its local allies and underpin the regional balance. In the short term there is no substitute for this role until there is a regional balance. In theory, such a balance is achievable. It could come about when the three main Gulf powers have rough military equality, as long as they are at the same time creating a functioning and flexible balance-of-power system. The concept of a 'security community' which envisages a functioning, interdependent region in which war is not only impracticable but unthinkable is also a possibility. This is the presumed end-point of a highly evolved model of a regional grouping of states that have experienced multiple wars and have transcended balance-of-power and even collective security systems as the means of organising their relations.

These developments are not likely in the foreseeable future. The US role is thus essential for Persian Gulf security, but it is also a role that needs careful consideration. How sustainable is it over time, especially in the face of domestic disorder in the Gulf? Can allied solidarity be maintained in the face of commercial pressures and differing interests or emphases? Above all, how can the current interim system be used to ensure an orderly transition to a self-sustaining regional one? How can the system now dominated by the United States do the least damage to building a future system?

Current US policy is predicated on the notion that only Iran and Iraq are hegemonic powers, not Saudi Arabia. Historically, this is a false proposition; indeed, the US has created a new order based on US–Saudi hegemony. This is most evident in the surge in Saudi military strength over time and a decline in those of Iran and Iraq. Given demographic and other factors, the sustainability of this state of affairs is questionable.[1]

Less debatable is the reaction of Iraq and Iran; neither will accept a state of affairs which ensures permanent inferiority. Neither of the wars involving Iraq (twice) and Iran were so clear-cut as to engender permanent lessons about the futility of war. Each ended murkily, with outside forces markedly tipping the balance. The positions of these states in the regional hierarchy remain open; they have certainly not shelved their own concepts of regional order or the role (if any) of outside powers in them. Both Iran and Iraq will have strong incentives to 'test' the artificial balance established by the United States and from which they are excluded. Iran's frequent military exercises and Iraq's feints – if feints they are – towards Kuwait demonstrate this. Each state, in the face of continued embargoes, may find the lure of WMDs correspondingly increased.

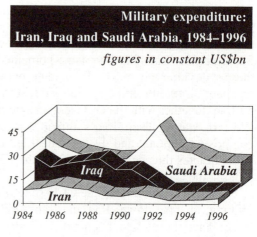

Military expenditure: Iran, Iraq and Saudi Arabia, 1984–1996

figures in constant US$bn

Note 1995 and 1996 figures are preliminary estimates
Source IISS, October 1996

The danger is that the US might seek to freeze the current order, making the construction of a durable system more difficult. Yet these states have to consider their future without a US presence. The East–West experience in arms control showed that progress was possible only when political relations improved and a prerequisite for that was dialogue. Arms-control agreements in turn deepened the political relationship. Dialogue and engagement between Iran and the GCC is specifically discouraged by the US. However, an atmosphere marked by territorial disputes, accusations of internal interference and fears of rearmament programmes does not lend much weight to efforts towards significant political progress, let alone to initiate some form of arms control.

The US connection is thus not an unmixed blessing. It enables Saudi Arabia to maintain its defensive and often hostile stance towards Iran (and Iraq), thereby avoiding the need to establish relations that may be necessary in the future. External security assistance from the US also helps the GCC as a whole to postpone indefinitely any politically sensitive decision on effective military integration. It simultaneously provides a continuing rationale for Saudi leadership and indeed for the existence of the GCC based on the spectre of external threats. Above all, it obscures the need for the GCC states to consider what type of relations it wants with their neighbours.

Nevertheless, the *pax Americana* could provide an opportunity to create a more solid structure for regional security. This will require prolonged contact and interaction among the three principal regional states. No viable structure can be built on the premise of excluding Iran and/or Iraq, but the three states agree neither on their respective regional roles, nor on the relative distribution of power. They clearly disagree on the baseline of any acceptable balance of power: Iran harks back to 1979, Iraq pines for 1988 and Saudi Arabia opts for the current balance as its starting point. Consequently, any accord among them will have to proceed by stages. In building confidence among these states, arms control will play an important although ancillary role. The first requisite is interaction in a regional forum that enables dialogue to begin. However unconstructive this might be at the outset, it can help blunt the politics of revenge and may also help to identify limited areas of agreement.

The most effective type of arms control in the Persian Gulf would be agreements that render more difficult a surprise attack on the land frontiers between Iran and Iraq and between Iraq and the GCC. Given the experiences of the past two decades, these are the most serious military scenarios; they are also susceptible to practical measures (unilateral if necessary, but bilateral if possible) which would increase warning time, through surveillance and monitoring, sparsely-manned and demilitarised zones. Similar agreements or confidence-building measures should also be possible at sea and in the air space between Iran and the GCC. Limited agreements should be not be difficult to reach, if they are part of a regional package that takes seriously the security needs of all states. To reach such agreements and to go beyond them to practical – regional – cooperation will take time. The time provided by the US umbrella could be used with this in mind to initiate rather than freeze dialogue.

However, the nature of that security umbrella and the view taken of it by the present regimes in Iraq and Iran place heavy responsibilities both on the regional states and, to some degree, on the US. For the Iranian government, the very presence of the US and its role in the Gulf inhibits dialogue on security cooperation with Saudi Arabia because it suggests acceptance of a status quo that Iran regards as deeply unsatisfactory and possibly threatening. It would be seen as surrendering to the reality of US power, something which no Iranian government would find easy. This must be recognised by the Saudi government and, if the latter is seriously interested in security cooperation, it must address the fears and insecurities of Tehran.

This presents the Saudi authorities with two different challenges. The first is to examine the many issues that arise in its bilateral relations with Iran and to find grounds for compromise rather than confrontation. The experience of the past few years has shown that deterioration of relations is always possible, but is not inevitable. Indeed, in some cases grounds for agreement existed, but were undermined in part by Saudi overreaction, caused possibly by a lack of detailed knowledge about the currents within the Iranian government and by general insecurity about its own position.

The second challenge is the Saudi handling of its relationship with the US. In this regard, there is little that Saudi Arabia can do to alter the perception of the US among Islamic radicals either in Iran or in Saudi Arabia itself. However, it can make an effort to dissociate this special security relationship from some of the areas of possible agreement with Iran. Or it might seek to demonstrate to Iran that this relationship and the logistical and technological back-up which it implies could work to the advantage of all states in the Gulf. This would in all likelihood require a measure of US approval, if not cooperation.

Against a background of deteriorating US–Iranian relations this will be a formidable challenge for Saudi Arabia. US adherence to the strategy of 'dual containment' since 1993, the trade embargo in force against Iran since 1995 and extended in 1996, as well as the US preoccupation with terrorism and Iran's role, make it difficult for Saudi Arabia to persuade Iran that any project in the Gulf taking place under the US security umbrella is not working against Iran's interests. Iranian reactions to threats of US military action or of covert operations within Iran will sabotage agreements reached with Saudi Arabia even in unconnected areas, precisely because of the tendency of Iranian Islamist radicals to stress the indivisibility of security issues.

The conclusion drawn from this is that the future of Saudi–Iranian relations and of a regional security system must depend on the state of US–Iranian relations, which will in turn be affected by domestic politics in Iran and by perceptions of Iran in the US. It is unlikely, in the present atmosphere, that the US will see beyond its peculiarly intimate animosity towards Iran to encourage rather than delay Saudi–Iranian dialogue and participate in its terms and aims. Were it able to do so, it might see the benefits that would accrue in the short-term from the formation of a regional forum. Unpalatable things might be said, but areas of concern could be addressed, ranging from the relatively neutral area of environmental issues to the highly charged questions of arms control. A model of sorts has already been provided in the Middle East by the Madrid conference.

In the long-term, the initiation of such a process could allay the anxieties which beset the US as it questions whether the Saudi state is strong enough to support its current balance of power strategy, and indeed whether that strategy may be weakening the very foundation it is intended to protect. Whilst there are few signs of such fundamental weakness at present in Saudi Arabia, there are concerns for the longer term security of the Kingdom if the sole barrier between it and a hostile region is the US alliance. This is a concern shared by some of the younger generation of the House of Saud and it is possible that only with their accession to power can Saudi Arabia chart a new course towards Iran.

Much however, will depend upon what happens in Iran itself. Clearly, if Saudi Arabia and the US face challenges in making overtures to Iran, the Iranian government itself faces an even greater challenge in making positive responses to such overtures. In the final analysis, it will be Iran's attitude to the US and by association to Saudi Arabia, which will influence the success of any attempt to create a regional security forum in the Gulf. In the present regional climate and condition of Iranian politics, the Iranian government's actions are more likely to encourage the maintenance of the very balance of power which they abhor. If it could be demonstrated – through incremental bilateral steps with Saudi Arabia, through greater openings from the GCC or through a regional forum – that there was a way of encouraging movement towards establishing a genuine regional security system, this might allow the pragmatically inclined members of the Iranian government to answer, although hardly to defeat, their more radical critics. Over time and with some positive achievements to show for such dialogue, growing confidence might permit other, presently unthinkable issues to be discussed. However, if current trends in US–Iranian relations continue, Saudi–Iranian relations are bound to suffer, exacerbating the many potential areas of bilateral conflict that already exist and reinforcing those on both sides who see no reason for dialogue across the Persian Gulf. This will in turn make any prospect of regional security cooperation more remote than ever.

NOTES

Chapter I

[1] See King Fahd's message to *Hajj* pilgrims, Saudi Arabian News Agency (SPA), BBC Summary of World Broadcasts, The Middle East (SWB/ME)/1107 A/1, 23 June in 25 June 1991.

[2] See the commentary on the GCC, 'An Anti-Iranian Pact', Islamic Republic News Agency (IRNA), Foreign Broadcast Information Service (FBIS)-SA-I-10-11, 16 October in 18 October 1982, p. 23.

[3] Hooshang Amirahmadi and Nader Entessar (eds), *Iran and the Arab World* (London: Macmillan, 1993), Amirahmadi, 'Iranian–Saudi Arabian Relations Since the Revolution', p. 149.

[4] Shahram Chubin, *Iran's National Security Policy: Capabilities, Intent and Impact* (Washington DC: Carnegie Endowment for International Peace, 1994).

[5] *Tehran Times* (editorial), 16 September 1989 in SWB/ME/0565 A/4, 19 September 1989.

[6] Jacob Goldberg, 'Saudi Arabia', *Middle East Contemporary Survey* (MECS), vol. 14, 1990, p. 614.

[7] Michael Renner, 'The Islamic Republic's Oil Policy' in Hooshang Amirahmadi and Manuchehr Parvin (eds), *Post-Revolutionary Iran* (Boulder, CO: Westview, 1988), pp. 190–197.

[8] These estimates, based on Central Bank of Iran data, are cited by Patrick Clawson, 'Islamic Iran's Economic Politics and Prospects', *The Middle East Journal*, vol. 42, no. 3, Summer 1988, pp. 377, 382.

[9] Hooshang Amirahmadi, 'Iran and the Persian Gulf Crisis' in Amirahmadi and Entessar (eds), *Iran and the Arab World*, p. 102.

[10] Amirahmadi, 'Iranian–Saudi Arabian Relations Since the Revolution', in *ibid.*, pp. 141, 144.

[11] 'A Conversation with Ambassador Hermann F. Eilts: The Dilemma in the Persian Gulf', *Studies in Foreign Policy* (Washington DC: American Enterprise Institute, May 1980), pp. 10–11. Even under the Shah the sectarian issue had not been absent in the relations of the two countries.

[12] Iran was unhappy with the Ta'if accord that ended the Lebanese civil war as much because it was Saudi-brokered as for its content. Shireen Hunter, 'Iran and Syria: From Hostility to Limited Alliance' in Amirahmadi and Entessar (eds), *Iran and the Arab World*, p. 210.

[13] Shireen Hunter, *Iran and the World: Continuity in a Revolutionary Decade* (Bloomington, IN: Indiana University Press, 1990), p. 123.

[14] Fred Halliday, 'Iranian Foreign Policy Since 1979: Internationalism and Nationalism in the Islamic Revolution' in R. I. Cole and Nikki R. Keddie (eds), *Shi'ism and Social Protest* (New Haven, CT: Yale University Press, 1986), pp. 106–7.

[15] See Rouhollah Ramazani, *Revolutionary Iran* (Baltimore, MD: The Johns Hopkins University Press, 1986), p. 92; Ramazani, 'Shi'ism in the Gulf' in Cole and Keddie, *Shi'ism and Social Protest*, pp. 30–54.

[16] Rouholla Ramazani, 'Khumayni's Islam in Iran's Foreign Policy' in Adeed Dawisha (ed.), *Islam in Foreign Policy* (Cambridge: Cambridge Univesity Press, 1983), p. 26.

[17] Joseph Kostiner, 'Shi'i Unrest in the Gulf' in Martin Kramer (ed.), *Shi'ism, Resistance and Revolution* (Boulder,

CO/London:Westview Press/Mansell, 1987), pp. 177–83.

[18] Mordechai Abir, *Saudi Arabia – Government, Society and the Gulf Crisis* (London: Routledge, 1993), pp. 112–13.

[19] Cited in Ramazani, 'Khumayni's Islam in Iran's Foreign Policy', p. 27.

[20] Voice of the IRI, 18 July 1990 in SWB/ME/0821 A/2, 20 July 1990.

[21] Speech by Rafsanjani at Tehran University, 17 June 1988 in SWB/ME/0182 A/6, 20 June 1988.

[22] Shahram Chubin, 'Post-War Gulf Security', *Survival,* vol. 33, no. 2, March/April 1991, pp. 140–57, and 'Iran and Regional Security in the Persian Gulf', *Survival,* vol. 34, no. 3, Autumn 1992, pp. 62-80.

[23] *Al-Riyadh,* 8 November 1990 in FBIS-NES-90-222, 16 November 1990, pp. 59–60.

Chapter II

[1] An understated characterisation of the US was that it was 'a major concern' to Iran. See Sohrab Shahabi and Farideh Farhi, 'Security Considerations in Iran's Foreign Policy', *The Iranian Journal of International Affairs,* vol. 7, no. 1, Spring 1995, p. 96.

[2] See the comment of Defence Minister Akbar Torkan who noted that Saudi Arabia outspent Iran more than twentyfold. Iran's defence expenditures in 1993 were $850m versus Saudi Arabia's $16.5bn. Voice of the IRI, 14 April 1993 in SWB/ME/1664 A/8, 16 April 1993.

[3] *Jomhuri-ye Eslami*, 3 November 1991 in SWB/ME/1221 A/2, 5 November 1991.

[4] See Hashemi Rafsanjani's address to the Conference on the Persian Gulf, Tehran, November 1989, in *Middle East Journal*, vol. 44, no. 3, Summer 1990, pp. 462, 465.

[5] The Chairman of the US Joint Chiefs of Staff, General John Shalikashvili, was quoted as saying this development 'bothered us very much'. *International Herald Tribune (IHT)*, 1 March 1995, p. 1. The Saudi reaction was cautious.

[6] See the comments of US Secretary of Defense William Perry before a visit to the Gulf , Kuwait News Agency (KUNA), 20 March 1995 in SWB/ME/2257 MED/17-18, 21 March 1995.

[7] *Sunday Times*, 20 February 1994, p. 6.

[8] *IHT*, 2 March 1995, p. 6. Iran's Deputy Head of Mission at the UN New York in a letter to the Secretary-General pledged a firm and strong response to any attempt to attack Iran's research centres. See Voice of the IRI, 7 February 1995 in SWB/ME/2223 MED/12, 9 February 1995.

[9] Sermon by Rafsanjani, Voice of the IRI, 8 March 1991 in SWB/ME/1017 A/11, 11 March 1991.

[10] See comments by Ayatollah Ali Khamene'i, Iranian radio and television, 27 October 1994 in SWB/ME/2138 MED/8-9, 28 October 1994.

[11] *Financial Times*, 2 September 1994, p. 4.

[12] *Al-Riyadh*, FBIS-NES-93-162, 16 August in 24 August 1993, pp. 23-24.

[13] Charles Tripp, 'The Gulf States and Iraq', *Survival*, vol. 34, no. 3, Autumn 1992, p. 50.

[14] Gulf News Agency (WAKH), 21 and 22 October 1991 in FBIS-NES-91-205, 23 October 1991, p. 1.

[15] Saudi Arabian Kingdom Radio Network, 14 January 1995 in FBIS-NES-95-013, 20 January 1995, p. 21.

[16] Saudi Arabian Television Network, 28 November 1994 in FBIS-NES-94-229, 29 November 1994, pp. 37–38.

[17] Saudi Arabian Television Network, 12 January 1993 in FBIS-NES-93-

008, 13 January 1993, p. 17.
[18] Saudi Arabian Television Network, 31 January 1993 in FBIS-NES-93-019, 1 February 1993, p. 22.
[19] See the conversation between King Fahd and the German Foreign Minister, Deutsche Presse-Agentur (DPA), 1 November 1993 in FBIS-NES-93-210, 2 November 1993, p. 33.
[20] See Shahram Chubin and Charles Tripp, 'Domestic Politics and Territorial Disputes in the Persian Gulf and Arabian Peninsula', *Survival,* vol. 35, no. 4, Winter 1993–94, pp. 4–27.
[21] See David Menashri, 'Iran', *MECS*, vol. 16, 1992, pp. 423–26.
[22] Chubin and Tripp, 'Domestic Politics and Territorial Disputes', *Survival*, pp. 4–27.
[23] See Prince Saud Bin Faisal's comments at the 50th session of the GCC Ministerial Council, Kingdom of Saudi Arabia, TV 1, 2 April 1994 in SWB/ME/1963 MED/9, 5 April 1994.
[24] Agence France-Presse (AFP), 26 March 1993 in FBIS-NES-93-059, 30 March 1993, p. 4.
[25] Saudi Arabian Television Network, 5 April 1993 in FBIS-NES-93-064, 6 April 1993, pp. 16–17.
[26] *Al-Sharq Al-Awsat*, 24 October 1994 in FBIS-NES-209, 28 October 1994, p. 19.
[27] For the GCC comments see KUNA, 18 September 1995 in SWB/ME/2413 MED/9, 20 September 1995.
[28] IRNA, 19 November 1995 in SWB/ME/2466 MED/12, 21 November 1995; WAKH and Voice of the IRI, 22 November 1995 in SWB/ME/2468 MED/14, 23 November 1995.
[29] Omani TV, 6 December 1995 in SWB/ME/2481 MED/1-2, 8 December 1995.
[30] See the comments of Ayatollah Mohammad Yazdi, Head of the Judiciary, Voice of the IRI, 23 September 1994 in SWB/ME/2110 MED/1, 26 September 1994.
[31] See the Commentary, Voice of the IRI, Network 1, 25 May 1994 in SWB/ME/2007 MED/7-8, 27 May 1994.
[32] The Foreign Ministry's declaration to this effect in response to the 15th summit of the GCC heads of state. Voice of the IRI, Network 1, 22 December 1994 in SWB/ME/2186 MED/10, 23 December 1994. Commentary, Voice of the IRI, 6 June 1995 in SWB/ME/2324 MED/9, 8 June 1995.
[33] See the Foreign Ministry statements, Voice of the IRI, Network 1, 4 April 1994 in SWB/ME/1965 MED/4, 7 April 1994.
[34] *Al-Hayat*, 11 January 1995 in FBIS-NES-95-008, 12 January 1995, p. 19; Middle East News Agency (MENA), 6 February 1995 in FBIS-NES-95-025, 7 February 1995, pp. 9–10.
[35] Voice of the IRI, 22 March 1995 in FBIS-NES-95-056, 23 March 1995, p. 38.
[36] David Menashri, *MECS*, vol. 16, 1992, p. 423.
[37] Quoted in *Ettela'at*, 26 December 1992; Radio Tehran, 25 December 1992. See *IHT*, 27 December 1992, p. 3. See also *Tehran Times*, 14 June 1995 in SWB/ME/2330 MED/1-2, 15 June 1995.
[38] SPA, 16 February 1996 in SWB/ME/2538 MED/16, 17 February 1996.
[39] See Voice of the IRI, 4 March 1995 in SWB/ME/2244 MED/9, 6 March 1995.
[40] IRNA, 26 April 1995 in SWB/ME/2289 MED/11-12, 28 April 1995.
[41] 'Riyad has no right to jeopardise Tehran–Manama relations', Commentary, Voice of IRI, 3 May in SWB/ME/2295 MED/4, 5 May 1995.
[42] See *Al-Quds Al-Arabi,* 12 December 1995 in SWB/ME/2486 MED/21, 14

December 1995.

[43] *IHT,* 22 January 1996, p. 8; *Le Monde,* 21-22 January 1996, p. 5. See also *Le Monde*, 23 January 1996, p. 3. For Bahraini newspaper accusations and Iranian media rebuttals, see SWB/ME/2516 MED/10-14, 23 January 1996.

[44] See *Al-Madinah* editorial as reported in *Financial Times,* 24 January 1996, p. 6; *The Economist*, 6 April 1996, p. 17.

[45] *IHT,* 22 June 1995, pp. 1, 7; *Financial Times*, 12 April 1996, p. 19; *Le Monde*, 21 May 1996, p. 5.

[46] For discussions of these themes, see Pirouz Mojtahed-Zadeh, 'A Geo-Political Triangle in the Persian Gulf: Actions and Reactions among Iran, Bahrain and Saudi Arabia', *Iranian Journal of International Affairs*, vol. 6, nos. 1 and 2, Spring/Summer 1994 pp. 54, 57.

[47] *Tehran Times* first reported that Iran was ready to defend the regional states from Saudi aggression, which it condemned. A later report disclosed that Rafsanjani might have offered to conclude a joint defence pact in a message to the Emir of Qatar. See respectively, *Tehran Times,* 3 October 1992 in SWB/ME/1503A/2, 5 October 1992; and Radio Monte Carlo, 3 October 1992 in SWB/ME/ 1504 A/2, 6 October 1992. See also comments by a senior Qatari official, *Al-Hayat*, 29 February 1996 in SWB/ ME/2550 MED/11, 2 March 1996.

[48] Witness Rafsanjani's comments, Voice of the IRI, Network 1, 9 April 1994 in SWB/ME/1968 MED/6, 11 April 1994.

[49] Saleh Al-Mani, 'Security and Threat Perceptions in Saudi Arabia', *National Threat Perceptions in the Middle East*, United Nations Institute for Disarmament Research Paper No. 37 (New York and Geneva: United Nations, 1995), p. 89.

[50] *Al-Yawm*, 6 December 1994 in FBIS-NES-94-237, 9 December 1994, p. 19.

[51] IRNA, 19 December 1994 in FBIS-NES-94-244, 20 December 1994, p. 19.

[52] See the comments by Mustafa Fumani, 'Roundtable', Vision of the IRI, Network 2, 7 April 1994 in SWB/ME/1968 MED/7, 11 April 1994.

[53] SPA, 15 December 1994 in FBIS-NES-94-241, 15 December 1994, p. 11.

[54] Voice of the IRI, Network 1, 27 February 1995 in SWB/ME/2239 MED/16-17, 28 February 1995.

[55] *Middle East Economic Survey* (*MEES*), vol. 39, no. 12, 18 December 1995, p. C2.

[56] See Iraqi News Agency (INA), 9 June 1996 in SWB/ME/2635 MED/ 17, 11 June 1996.

[57] Iran's Supreme National Security Council expressed this as official policy. Commentary, Voice of the IRI, 23 August 1992 in SWB/ME/1468 A/ 8-9, 25 August 1992, and Kingdom of Saudi Arabia radio, 26 August 1992 in SWB/ME/1471 A/2, 28 August 1992.

[58] See the extracts from the Saudi press quoted in SPA, 15 January 1993 in FBIS-NES-93-012, 19 January 1993, p. 21.

[59] Tripp, 'The Gulf States and Iraq', pp. 54–55.

[60] Saudi Arabian Television Network, 2 April 1994 in FBIS-NES-94-064, 4 April 1994, p. 25.

[61] Kuwait Television, 12 October 1994 in FBIS-NES-94-198, 13 October 1994, p. 32.

[62] KUNA, 21 December 1994 in FBIS-NES-94-245, 21 December 1994, p. 42.

[63] Based on discussions at the non-aligned conference, Iranian Foreign

Minister Ali Akbar Vellayati reported that the positions are similar. Vision of the IRI, Network 2, 9 June 1994 in SWB/ME/2020 MED/7-8, 13 June 1994.

[64] *The Economist*, 29 May 1993, p. 42.

[65] See Vellayati's comments, IRNA, 29 June 1991 in SWB/ME/1113 A/8, 2 July 1991.

[66] Ayatollah Khamene'i, 21 January 1993 in SWB/ME/1592i, 26 January 1993.

[67] Commentary, Voice of the IRI, 6 May 1993 in SWB/ME/1683 A/4-5, 8 May 1993.

[68] Voice of the IRI, 27 June 1993 in SWB/ME/1727 A/3, 29 June 1993.

[69] *IHT*, 29 March 1993, p. 2.

[70] Vellayati on a visit to Oman, Jordanian TV, 6 September 1994 in SWB/ME/2096 MED/5, 9 September 1994.

[71] See Commentary, Voice of the IRI, 22 May 1994 in SWB/ME/2311 MED/10-11, 24 May 1994.

[72] Ali Khorram, adviser to the Foreign Minister, Vision of the IRI, Network 2, 1 June 1994 in SWB/ME/2320 MED/9-10, 3 June, 1994.

[73] See Hasan Ruhani, Secretary of the Supreme National Security Council, IRNA, 18 July 1995 in SWB/ME/2360 MED/1-2, 20 July 1995.

[74] IRNA, 13 February 1996 in SWB/ME/2535 MED/4, 14 February 1996.

[75] INA, 13 February 1993 in SWB/ME/2228 MED/1, 15 February, 1993; Voice of the IRI, 8 August 1993 in SWB/ME/1762 A/7-8, 9 August 1993.

[76] *Tehran Times*, 21 February 1995 in SWB/ME/1928 MED/5, 22 February 1995. Iran formally informed the UN Secretary-General that it holds Iraq responsible for the actions of the Mujahedin. IRNA, 21 June 1994 in SWB/ME/2029 MED/8, 23 June 1994.

[77] Its leader, Baqir Al-Hakim, denied any reduction in support despite the Iran–Iraq dialogue. Radio Monte Carlo, 23 July 1995 in SWB/ME/2364 MED/16-17, 25 July 1995.

[78] *New York Times*, 20 March 1991, pp. 1, 12.

[79] See INA, 28 November 1992 in SWB/ME/1551 A/11-12, 30 November 1992.

[80] *Al-Thawra*, 11 June 1995 in SWB/ME/2327 MED/15-16, 12 June 1995.

[81] *Al Thawra*, 16 April 1992 in SWB/ME/1359 A/20, 20 April 1992.

[82] Saddam Hussein, Republic of Iraq radio, 8 September 1992 in SWB/ME/1482 A/3, 10 September 1992, and Republic of Iraq radio, speech to mark second anniversary of start of 1991 Gulf War, 17 January 1993 in SWB/ME/1590 A/2, 19 January 1993.

[83] Army Day speech by Saddam Hussein, Republic of Iraq radio, 5 January 1994 in SWB/ME/1889 MED/9, 7 January 1994, and speech marking fourth anniversary of 1991 Gulf War, Republic of Iraq radio, 7 January 1995 in SWB/ME/2205 MED/6, 19 January 1995.

[84] Tariq Aziz, INA, 12 April 1991 in SWB/ME/1046 A/3, 15 April 1991. Saddam Hussein's speech commemorating the seventh anniversary of the recapture of the Faw peninsula, Iraqi TV, 8 August 1995 in SWB/ME/2377 MED/5-10, 9 August 1995.

[85] See *Al-Thawra*, 20 December 1993 in SWB/ME/1877 MED/5, 21 December 1993, and *Al-Thawra*, 10 July 1995 in SWB/ME/2352 MED/9, 11 July 1995.

[86] INA, 4 September 1995 in SWB/ME/2400 MED/1, 5 September 1995.

[87] In a CNN interview carried by INA, 26 January 1993 in SWB/ME/1598 A/2-3, 28 January 1993.

[88] See, for example, *Abrar* and *Tehran Times*, 21 February 1994, which see

Iraq as training Iranian dissidents while calling for better relations – in short 'playing a double game'. IRNA, 21 February 1994 in SWB/ME/1928 MED/5, 22 February 1994.

[89] *MEES,* vol. 39, no. 2, 9 October 1995, pp. C2-3.

[90] IRNA, 13 February 1996 in SWB/ME/2535 MED/4, 14 February 1996; IRNA, 12 February 1996 in SWB/ME/2535 MED/6, 14 February 1996; *Al-Hayat,* 16 February 1996.

[91] *Al-Thawra,* 18 February 1996 in SWB/ME/2540 MED/7, 20 February 1996.

[92] Saudi Crown Prince Abdullah Bin Abd Al-Aziz, SPA, 4 December in SWB/ME/2478 MED/2, 5 December 1995.

[93] Hasan Ruhani, Iranian TV, 14 December 1995 in SWB/ME/2488 MED/6-8, 16 December 1995.

Chapter III

[1] Ayatollah Ahmad Jannati, at Tehran University mosque. 26 March 1993 in Voice of the IRI, SWB/ME/1649 A/3-5, 29 March 1993.

[2] *Al-Hayat,* 24 April 1994 in FBIS-NES-94-080, 26 April 1994, p. 16–17.

[3] SPA, 1 June 1993 in FBIS-NES-93-104, 2 June 1993, p. 20.

[4] See especially the chapters on Iran by Menashri, *MECS,* vol. 15, 1991, and *MECS,* vol. 16, 1992.

[5] SPA, 15 March 1994 in FBIS-NES-94-051, 16 March 1994, p. 11.

[6] As Menashri argues in 'Iran', *MECS,* vol. 15, 1991 .

[7] See references by Iranian commentator Bahman Bakhtiari, 'Revolutionary Iran's Persian Gulf Policy: The Quest for Regional Supremacy', Amirahmadi and Entessar (eds), *Iran and the Arab World*, especially pp. 81–83. Note also the editors' introductory reference to Iran's 'volatile' policy in the Persian Gulf since the revolution, pp. 4–5.

[8] See Mohammad Taqi Jafari, *Jomhuri-ye Eslami,* 11 June 1992 in SWB/ME/1406 A/5, 13 June 1992.

[9] IRNA, 26 May 1993 in SWB/ME/1700A/10, 28 May 1993.

[10] *The Guardian,* 30 October 1993, p. 7.

[11] Former Interior Minister, Ali Akhbar Motashemi, Interview with Radio Monte Carlo, 11 June 1993 in SWB/ME/1714 A/4, 14 June 1993.

[12] Voice of the IRI, 23 July 1990 in SWB/ME/0825A/6, 25 July 1990.

[13] Comments to *Ettela'at*, IRNA, 22 April 1991 in SWB/ME/1054 A/4, 24 April 1991.

[14] R. Hrair Dekmejian, 'The Rise of Political Islamism in Saudi Arabia', *The Middle East Journal,* vol. 48, no. 4, Autumn 1994, especially pp. 639–642.

[15] Joshua Teitelbaum, 'Saudi Arabia', *MECS,* vol. 16, 1992, p. 683.

[16] *The Guardian*, 8 May 1993, 10 May 1993; *The Independent*, 14 May 1993; *Le Monde*, 18 May 1993.

[17] IRNA, 2 June 1993 in FBIS-NES-93-104, 2 June 1993, p. 18.

[18] SPA, 2 June 1993 in FBIS-NES-93-105, 3 June 1993, p. 15.

[19] SPA, 1 May 1994 in FBIS-NES-94-084, 2 May 1994, p. 40.

[20] IRNA, 16 May 1994 in FBIS-NES-94-095, 17 May 1994, p. 20.

[21] Message to the *Hajj*, Voice of the IRI, Network 1, 20 April 1994 in SWB/ME/1978 MED/7-9, 22 April 1994 (emphasis added).

[22] Ayatollah Meshkini, senior member of Assembly of Experts, Vision of IRI, Network 2, 28 May 1994 in SWB/ME/2010 MED/7, 31 May 1994.

[23] Vision of IRI, Network 1, 20 April 1994 in SWP/ME/1978 MED/10, 22 April 1994; Vision of the IRI, Network 1, 20 May 1994 in SWB/

ME/2004 MED/12-13, 23 May 1994; Vision of the IRI, Network 1, 31 May 1994 in SWB/ME 2011 MED/7, 1 June 1994.

[24] Voice of the IRI, 1 May 1995 in SWB/ME/2293 MED/4-5, 3 May 1995.

[25] Note Menashri's view that the *Hajj* is 'more barometer than cause' of the state of relations. *MECS*, vol. 15, 1991, p. 405.

[26] IRNA, 12 November 1995 in SWB/ME/2459 MED/6, 13 November 1995.

[27] Khamene'i consistently refers to it as 'the main problem of the Islamic world'. Rafsanjani has summarised the issue as follows: 'The Palestine question is an Islamic one and we have a say in it. We are involved. It is our right to demand [that] an injustice has been committed and has to be corrected'. Press Conference, 31 January 1992 in SWB/ME/1604 A/12, 4 February 1993.

[28] Menashri, *MECS*, vol. 15, 1991, pp. 409–10. See also Chubin, *Iran's National Security Policy*, pp. 11–15.

[29] Sermon by Rafsanjani, Tehran University, Voice of the IRI, 19 March 1993 in SWB/ME/1643 A/1-5, 22 March 1993.

[30] Speech by Khamene'i at Mashad, and Vision of the IRI, 24 March and 25 March 1993 respectively, SWB/ME/1648 A/1, 27 March 1993.

[31] Khamene'i, Voice of IRI, 28 April 1993 in SWB/ME/1676 A/9-11, 30 April 1993.

[32] See Voice of the IRI, 2 October 1994 in SWB/ME/2116 MED/2, 3 October 1994.

[33] Khamene'i, 'Iran Leader Warns Arabs over Peace with Israel', *IHT*, 28 October 1994, p. 5.

[34] IRI and IRNA, 22 December and 27 December 1994, respectively, in SWB/ME/2188 MED/1-3, 29 Decem-

ber 1994.

[35] *Al-Sharq Al-Awsat*, 23 September 1993 in FBIS-NES-93-187, 29 September 1993, p. 21.

[36] The critics themselves, exemplified by Dr Muhammad Al-Mas'ari, were outraged by Sheikh Bin Baz' *fatwa*. See the interview with Voice of the IRI, 1 May 1995 in FBIS-NES-95-084, 2 May 1995, p. 37.

[37] SPA, 26 October 1994 in FBIS-NES-94-207, 26 October 1994, p. 24.

[38] Radio Pakistan Network, 11 March 1993 in FBIS-NES-93-046, 11 March 1993, p. 25; SPA, 12 March 1993 in FBIS-NES-93-047, 12 March 1993, p. 28.

[39] SPA, 4 October 1994 in FBIS-NES-94-192, 4 October 1994, p. 31.

[40] Menashri, *MECS*, vol. 16, 1992, p. 419.

[41] See Martin Kramer, 'Rallying Around Islam', *MECS*, vol. 17, 1993, p. 129.

[42] Ayatollah Khamene'i noted that Iran was not 'duty bound' to fight in *jihad* on the issue; it was too far away. See speech in Babol, Voice of the IRI, Network 1, 17 October 1995 in SWB/ME/2438 MED/12, 19 October 1995.

[43] Al-Mani, 'Security and Threat Perceptions', p. 91.

Chapter IV

[1] The costs of the Gulf War for Saudi Arabia have been estimated at $37.5bn, although some Saudi sources have claimed that the costs were higher. Oil revenue during this period was estimated at $39.5bn, Joseph Kostiner, 'Saudi Arabia', *MECS,* vol. 15, 1991, p. 623.

[2] *NewYork Times*, 13 September 1993, pp. D1–D2.

[3] *Financial Times* quotes 58%, 27 June 1995, p. 3.

[4] Patrick Clawson, 'Alternative Foreign Policy Views Among the

Iranian Foreign Policy Elite', Patrick Clawson (ed.), *Iran's Strategic Intentions,* McNair Paper 29, (Washington DC: National Defense University, 1994), pp. 33–37.

[5] See Fereidun Fesharaki's comment, *New York Times*, 3 April 1994, p. 3.

[6] Rafsanjani's inauguration speech on his second presidential term at the Majlis, Voice of the IRI, 4 August 1993 in SWB/ME/1760 A/6, 6 August 1993.

[7] Note the comments by the Oil Minister, SWB/ME/2347 MED/12, 5 July 1995.

[8] Especially since Iraq wants to make up for lost time and seeks to export 6 mb/d, according to Iraqi Oil Minister, Safa Hadi Jawad, INA, 23 May 1995 in SWB/ME/2311 MED/11, 24 May 1995.

[9] See Hooshang Amirahmadi, 'Iran and the Persian Gulf: Strategic Issues and Outlook', *Iranian Journal of International Affairs,* vol. 5, no. 2, Summer 1993, pp. 385, 387, 401.

[10] *Financial Times*, 29 March 1994, p. 16; Teitelbaum, 'Saudi Arabia', *MECS*, vol. 16, 1992, p. 690.

[11] *Sunday Times*, 27 June 1993, p.11, and *IHT*, 1 April 1994, p. 6. (The editorial talks of the Saudis 'returning the favor' for US military assistance.)

[12] For background, see David Rachovich, 'Middle East Oil Developments', *MECS*, vol. 15, 1991, pp. 277–300, and *MECS*, vol. 16, 1992, pp. 313–334 .

[13] *Financial Times*, 26 July 1993, p. 1; *IHT*, 26 July 1993, p. 7; *Le Monde*, 9 June 1993, p. 20; *Financial Times*, 26 November 1993, p. 1. In the new setting *market share* assumed more importance than price.

[14] *IHT*, 30 September 1993, pp. 1, 17.

[15] AFP, FBIS-NES-93-185, 27 September in 27 September 1993, p. 16.

[16] *Tehran Times*, IRNA, 11 January 1994 in SWB/ME/1894 MED/9, 13 January 1994.

[17] Voice of the IRI, 16 January 1994 in FBIS-NES-94-011, 18 January 1994, p. 73.

[18] *Tehran Times*, 23 February 1994 in SWB/ME/1930 MED/3-4, 24 February 1994.

[19] Saudi Oil Ministry statement, 18 March in SPA, FBIS-NES-94-054, 21 March 1994, p. 24.

[20] According to the Oil Minister Gholam Reza Aghazadeh. Voice of the IRI, Network 1, 26 March 1994 in SWB/ME/1957 MED/4, 28 March 1994.

[21] Hojjat el Eslam Mostafa Ha'eri Fumani, Director General, Persian Gulf desk, Foreign Ministry, 'Political Roundtable', Vision of IRI, Network 2, 26 March 1994 in SWB/ME/1968 MED/6-8, 11 April 1994.

[22] The Saudi position was given by King Fahd and Crown Prince Abdullah in their message to pilgrims, SPA, 22 May 1994 in SWB/ME/2005 MED/9, 24 May 1994.

Conclusion

[1] Iranian media and officials claimed that the bomb explosion in Riyadh in November 1995 and Al-Khobar in June 1996 in which numbers of US service personnel were killed underlined both the level of popular dissatisfaction with US 'hegemonic policies' and showed up this fragility, based as they are on limited Saudi capabilities. Voice of the IRI, 12 November 1995 in SWB/ME 2461 MED/4, 15 November 1995; Hojjat Al-Eslam Khonsari, Radio Monte Carlo, 28 June 1996 in SWB/ME/ 2652 MED/9-10,1 July 1996.